Study Guide

for

Muchinsky's

Psychology Applied to Work

Eighth Edition

Marc C. Marchese
Kings College

THOMSON

WADSWORTH

Australia • Brazil • Canada • Mexico • Singapore • Spain • United Kingdom • United States

ISBN 0-495-03050-3

Thomson Higher Education
10 Davis Drive
Belmont, CA 94002-3098
USA

For more information about our products, contact us at:
Thomson Learning Academic Resource Center
1-800-423-0563

For permission to use material from this text or product, submit a request online at
http://www.thomsonrights.com.
Any additional questions about permissions can be submitted by email to **thomsonrights@thomson.com.**

TABLE OF CONTENTS

CHAPTER 1: The Historical Background of I/O Psychology

CHAPTER 2: Research Methods in I/O Psychology

CHAPTER 3: Criteria: Standards for Making Decisions

CHAPTER 4: Predictors: Psychological Assessments

CHAPTER 5: Personnel Decisions

CHAPTER 6: Organizational Learning

CHAPTER 7: Performance Management

CHAPTER 8: Organizations and Organizational Change

CHAPTER 9: Teams and Teamwork

CHAPTER 10: Organizational Attitudes and Behavior

CHAPTER 11: Occupational Health

CHAPTER 12: Work Motivation

CHAPTER 13: Leadership

CHAPTER 14: Union/Management Relations

Author Note

Marc C. Marchese received his Ph.D. in Industrial/Organizational Psychology from Iowa State University in 1992. Currently, he is an associate professor and director of the human resources management program at King's College in Wilkes-Barre, Pennsylvania. He has taught courses in industrial psychology, training and development, psychological testing, graduate and undergraduate introduction to HRM, organizational theory, employment and labor law, and organizational communication. His research interests include employee mentoring, job enrichment, part-time/full-time employee differences, and personnel selection.

Preface

      This study guide was designed to be used with Muchinsky's eighth edition of Psychology Applied to Work. For each chapter, the study guide begins with an outline of **key terms and concepts**. You could use the outline either to take notes when reading the text or you could use the outline to quiz yourself when preparing for exams. The guide then presents the critical concepts visually in the form of **concept charts**. Next, the study guide has a listing of the relevant **web sites** for the text chapters. You could use these web sites as starting points for course assignments and exercises. Moreover, each chapter in the study guide presents a variety of interesting **exercises**. The objective of these exercises is to help you apply and understand the material presented in class and in the textbook. Lastly, to help you further prepare for exams, each chapter has ten **multiple-choice questions**, five **true-false questions** and three **short-answer questions**. The **answers** for the multiple–choice items and true-false items are also provided.

I would like to thank Jessica Milbrodt for her helpful ideas to improve this manual.

I hope you find this study guide valuable as you complete this course. Good luck!

Sincerely,

Marc C. Marchese, Ph.D.
Associate Professor of HRM
King's College

Chapter 1: Study Guide

THE HISTORICAL BACKGROUND OF I/O PSYCHOLOGY

Chapter 1: Outline

The following is a list of key names, terms and concepts from Chapter 1. As a way to help you understand the chapter and get to know the material, go through each of the terms and describe them fully. Then compare your responses to the responses in the textbook.

Note that you should not rely solely on key term lists when studying for your class exams. Instead, you should go back and make sure you thoroughly understand the content of the chapters and the content of your class notes.

Psychology

       APA

       APS

Industrial/Organizational Psychology

       Division 14 of the APA

       SIOP

       Two sides of I/O Psychology: Science versus practice

       FOUR main work settings of I/O Psychologists

Fields of I/O Psychology (Can you see how they are different?)

       Selection and Placement

       Training and Development

Performance Appraisal

Organization Development

Quality of Work Life

Ergonomics

Licensing of Psychologists

Licensing law

Purpose of licensing

Controversy regarding licensure of I/O Psychologists

The Early Years of I/O Psychology (1900-1916)

W.L. Bryan

Walter Dill Scott

Frederick W. Taylor

Lillian Moller Gilbreth

Hugo Munsterberg

World War I (1917-1918)

Robert Yerkes

Army Alpha

Army Beta

Journal of Applied Psychology

Between the Wars (1919-1940)

       Bureau of Salesmanship Research

       Psychological Corporation

       James Cattell

       Hawthorne studies

       Hawthorne effect

World War II (1941-1945)

       Army General Classification Test (AGCT)

       Situational stress tests

       Selection and training of pilots

       Value of the world wars for I/O psychology

Toward Specialization (1946-1963)

       Development of college programs in I/O psychology

       Engineering psychology

       Elton Mayo

       Personnel psychology

       Human relations movement

Governmental Intervention (1964-1993)

       Title VII of the Civil Rights Act of 1964

       Americans with Disabilities Act of 1990

       Civil Rights Act of 1991

Family and Medical Leave Act of 1991

Project A

ASVAB

The Information Age (1994-Present)

The impact of change

E-business

Chief information officer

I/O psychology and 9/11/01

Cross-Cultural I/O Psychology

Cross-cultural psychology

The impact of globalization

Language differences

Time spent at work across countries

The Mandate of I/O Psychology

Increase the fit between the workforce & the workplace in a time of rapid change

Workforce trends

Industry trends

Societal trends

Concept Charts for Chapter 1

Four Main Work Areas for I/O Psychologists

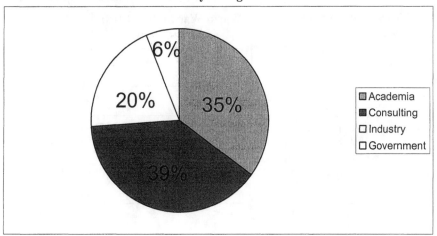

Six Fields of I/O Psychology

Selection & Placement	Training & Development	Performance Appraisal
Organizational Development	Quality of Work Life	Ergonomics

The History of I/O Psychology

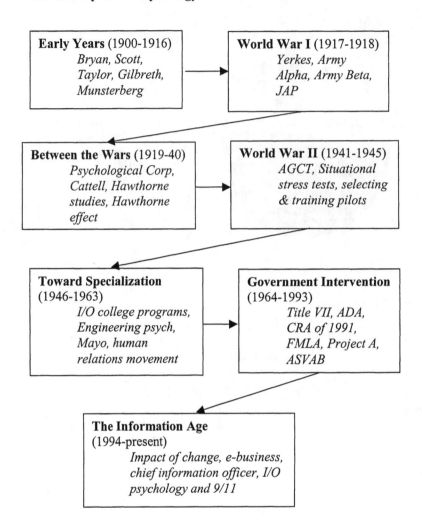

Early Years (1900-1916)
Bryan, Scott, Taylor, Gilbreth, Munsterberg

World War I (1917-1918)
Yerkes, Army Alpha, Army Beta, JAP

Between the Wars (1919-40)
Psychological Corp, Cattell, Hawthorne studies, Hawthorne effect

World War II (1941-1945)
AGCT, Situational stress tests, selecting & training pilots

Toward Specialization (1946-1963)
I/O college programs, Engineering psych, Mayo, human relations movement

Government Intervention (1964-1993)
Title VII, ADA, CRA of 1991, FMLA, Project A, ASVAB

The Information Age (1994-present)
Impact of change, e-business, chief information officer, I/O psychology and 9/11

Web Sites for Chapter 1

Here are some general I/O psychology and human resources web sites that may be beneficial to you throughout this course.

1) http://www.siop.org/

    This is the SIOP web site.

2) http://www.apa.org/

    This web site is the American Psychological Association.

3) http://www.siop.org/TIP/TIP.html

    This web site has TIP (The Industrial Psychologist) on-line.

4) http://www.psychologicalscience.org/about/links.html

    This web site is the home page for the American Psychological Society.

5) http://www.shrm.org

    This is the web site for the Society of Human Resources Management.

Exercise 1-1: Applying I/O Psychology to Your Last Job

The first chapter of your textbook introduced you to the field and history of I/O Psychology. If someone would ask you what an I/O psychologist does, could you answer him or her now? If not, you should review the chapter once again. Also realize your ideas of what an I/O psychologist does will become more concrete and better defined as you continue through your I/O psychology course. As described in the book, an I/O psychologist may be concerned with a wide variety of organizational issues. Following are some of the things an I/O psychologist might do:

* write job descriptions so that employees and managers are clear about job responsibilities
* create performance appraisal forms to assess how workers are doing on the job
* develop training programs to help workers learn and improve on the job
* develop selection tests to help managers select the best-qualified individual for a position
* conduct job satisfaction surveys to see if workers are satisfied with their jobs
* conduct research to understand problems of turnover, absenteeism, and motivation
* design methods to improve communication between workers and management
* improve work environments for workers
* improve productivity by job redesign
* attempt to reduce work stress among employees

This exercise will make you think about how I/O psychology might be used in the last job you held (or are working at right now). Then, as you continue learning about I/O psychology, you can keep the example of the last job you held (or the job you are working at right now) in your mind. If you have never held a job, please ask a roommate, friend, or family member to help you complete this exercise.

1.   Describe the most recent job that you have held (or a job you are working at currently). What types of duties did your job entail?

2.   What might an I/O psychologist do in the organization that you worked for? List at least five things. For example, if you were not trained very well when you started your job, you might suggest that an I/O psychologist come

8

in and evaluate how workers were trained. Please be very specific and give some explanation.

Exercise 1-2: SIOP & Student Membership

Becoming a student affiliate of the Society for Industrial and Organizational Psychology (SIOP)

It may be of interest to a small number of you taking this industrial/organizational psychology course to pursue knowledge in this field further. You may, for example, want to become a student affiliate of SIOP. Recall from your textbook that "SIOP" is Division 14 of APA and is also known as the Society for Industrial/Organizational Psychology. While professional members of SIOP are required to also belong to APA or APS, student members can join SIOP without belonging to APA or APS. An individual applying for student affiliate status in SIOP does not need to be majoring in psychology, but must have a faculty member sign to verify that he or she is a student in good standing and is engaged in study related to I/O psychology.

As a student member of SIOP, you will receive a subscription to The Industrial-Organizational Psychologist (known as "TIP"). This publication will give you information about job opportunities in I/O Psychology (usually for Ph.D. level applicants), recent legal issues relevant to the workplace, SIOP's annual conference held in the spring of each year, and other information that professionals in the I/O field need. Because TIP is written for professionals in the I/O field, you may only be interested in its content if your career goal is to work in this area.

Student membership in SIOP is only $25. In order to be accepted into SIOP as a student member, you need to FILL OUT A STUDENT APPLICATION FORM. Go to: http://www.siop.org/student_affiliate.html

Becoming a student member of the Society for Human Resource Management

Another national organization students might find appealing is known as the Society for Human Resource Management, or SHRM. SHRM is a much larger organization than SIOP, and includes individuals with a background in human resources. You are eligible for student membership if (1) you are enrolled in at least six semester hours (or eight quarter hours) per term and (2) if your planned or completed coursework supports a demonstrated interest in human resource management. You do not have to be planning on graduate school to benefit from this organization.

Student members of SHRM receive several benefits, including a monthly magazine (HRMagazine) and newsletter (HRNews). HRMagazine includes in-depth articles on several applied human resource management issues, such as performance appraisal, training, compensation, and sexual harassment. HRNews is a great resource for job openings in human resources and legal updates on human resource issues. Student membership in SHRM may be more appropriate than TIP (described previously) for students who want to work in human resources without a M.S. or Ph.D. In general, SHRM publications tend to be more applied in nature than SIOP publications.

Student membership in SHRM is $35.00. Because SHRM is a large national organization, there may be a local chapter of SHRM near you that has regular meetings. Your university may even have a student chapter with a faculty advisor. For more information about joining SHRM, go to: http://www.shrm.org/students/memberinfo.asp

---

Exercise 1-3: Graduate School in I/O Psychology

Your textbook will introduce you to the exciting field of Industrial/Organizational (I/O) Psychology. The concepts you learn in this class (e.g., about job analysis, selection, performance appraisal, training workers, motivating workers, job satisfaction, job design, stress in the workplace, unions, etc.) will be a tremendous help to you professionally *no matter what your major or career interest*. Most students that take industrial/ organizational psychology as a class, in fact, are not planning to practice I/O Psychology but will use the concepts they learn in the course in their own respective fields.

Nevertheless, some of you may be interested in pursuing I/O Psychology as a career specialty. For those individuals, this exercise will lead you through the steps for finding out more information about graduate school opportunities in the field. As discussed in the book, a graduate education (M.S. or Ph.D.) is necessary to practice as an I/O Psychologist. It should be noted, however, that some individuals are able to find jobs in a human resources department with a B.S. or B.A. degree in psychology and a strong emphasis in industrial psychology or business.

Graduate school is not for everyone! Admission into graduate programs is competitive, admitting only students that have a high grade point average, good GRE scores (an admission test you must take to get into most graduate programs in psychology), research experience, and strong letters of recommendation. Masters programs typically take two years, including summers. Ph.D. programs typically take students between four and six years to complete. Students should really like to read and study, and at the Ph.D. level, they should be willing to take several statistics courses and do multiple research projects. Although M.S. programs tend to be more application-oriented and Ph.D. programs tend to be more research-oriented, both types of programs usually follow a research/practitioner model where both science and practice are emphasized.

If you are interested in learning more about applying for graduate school in I/O Psychology, this exercise will be very helpful for you. Read and complete the following steps. I also strongly encourage you to discuss your interests with a faculty member. Discussing your interests with a faculty member will help you determine whether or not graduate school is appropriate for you.

Steps to Complete

1. Take at least one course in I/O Psychology to make sure the field interests you. Ask your instructor questions about career opportunities in I/O Psychology. As discussed in the book, there are opportunities in industry, consulting, government, and academia. Career options differ depending on whether you earn a M.S. or Ph.D. What career options in I/O appeal to you? Write them here.

2. Meet with faculty members to discuss what classes you should be taking to best prepare yourself for graduate work in I/O Psychology. It is helpful for individuals who want a Ph.D. in I/O Psychology to have a strong quantitative and science background. It is also helpful, although not necessary, for individuals to have taken several I/O or business-related courses. List all quantitative (math, statistics, computer, or research methods), science, I/O, and business-related courses you have taken:
    Quantitative:
    Science:
    Business-related:

3. Faculty members typically advise their students to apply for at least five different graduate programs. You will thus need to know where there are graduate programs available in I/O Psychology. A great place to find information on graduate programs in I/O psychology is at the following web site from SIOP:

    http://www.siop.org/GTP/

Request information from all prospective schools to which you might apply. Ideally, this should be done about one year before you hope to attend graduate school. Simply send a postcard to each I/O program you are interested in and ask them to send you information about their program and admission standards. List the programs that interest you or that you wrote to for information here:

4. Most graduate programs require that you take the GRE. Your scores on the GRE will be interpreted as a measure of your general intellectual ability along with your grade point average. There are books available at most books stores that will help you to prepare for the GRE. It is recommended that you take the GRE during October of the year before the academic year you want to start graduate school. There is usually an academic assistance center or placement center at most universities where you can get information about registering to take the GRE. Otherwise, you can call ETS at 609-921-9000 and ask about registration fees and test dates.

5. For most Ph.D. programs in I/O, you will need to complete the applications for admissions in December or January before the August in which you would like admission. Masters' program deadlines are typically later. You will usually need to write a letter of intention (or a personal statement) to include with your applications. It should be carefully typed, and should include information about your career goals and what you have done to prepare yourself for graduate school. You should be able to convince the person reading the letter that you are very interested in obtaining a graduate degree in this field, and that you are a qualified and motivated applicant. List some thoughts you will want to include in your personal statement here:

6. You will also need letters of recommendation from faculty in your department. Ideally, you will have been working on research with at least one of your instructors, so that this instructor can write a letter saying that you have research experience. Be organized and ask for letters of recommendation a month or more before they are due. Provide your recommender with stamped envelopes with the appropriate addresses typed on them to facilitate the process. Make sure to provide your recommender with the dates that the recommendations are due.

You have just taken several of the important steps in your process of considering and applying for graduate school. I wish you the best of luck with your decision about what you want to do with your future. It is important to think about your future career goals and how to prepare yourself to reach them. Consult your academic advisor with any questions you may have.

Self-Test for Chapter 1

Sample multiple-choice items:

1) Division 14 of the APA represents I/O psychologists. This division is called:

   a) JAP
   b) SIOP
   c) SHRM
   d) ASVAB

2) The field of I/O psychology that would most likely examine the stress of machines and equipment on employees is called:

   a) quality of worklife
   b) ergonomics
   c) organizational development
   d) training and development

3) The present stage in the history of I/O psychology is referred to as:

   a) Government intervention
   b) Toward specialization
   c) The information age
   d) Technological change

4) Which of the following is not a founding father of I/O psychology?

   a) W. L. Bryan
   b) Walter Dill Scott
   c) Frederick Taylor
   d) Hugo Munsterberg

5) Which of the following tests were used during World War I?

   a) Army beta
   b) Army general classification test
   c) Situational stress test
   d) Armed services vocational aptitude battery

6) A local company decided to give its employees a chance to voice their opinions through the use of a suggestion box. Employees initially appreciated this opportunity and the productivity in the plant increased significantly. After a few months, however, the novelty of the suggestion box wore out and employees returned to previous levels of performance. This is an example of:

a) organizational development
b) the Hawthorne effect
c) engineering psychology
d) the human relations movement

7) The human relations movement:

a) examined social relationships in the work environment
b) focused on improving work efficiency through specialization
c) emphasized careful selection procedures
d) was the guiding force in completing Project A

8) The main goal of title VII of the Civil Rights Act of 1964 was:

a) encourage the use of tests in the selection procedure
b) reduce unfair discrimination against minorities
c) reduce compensation disparities between men and women
d) prohibit age discrimination in the workplace

9) In response to 9/11/01, I/O psychologists played a vital role in:

a) identifying key cultural indicators of potential terrorists
b) classifying employees who may likely commit violent acts
c) documenting the workplace stressors in airports and seaports
d) assisting the TSA in selecting airport security screeners

10) The mandate of I/O psychology is to:

a) increase the fit between the workplace and the workforce in a time of rapid change
b) improve work-life balance for employees
c) increase compensation for the middle class worker
d) make jobs more enjoyable and creative

14

Sample true-false items:

1) Approximately 25% of all psychologists are in the I/O area. T-or-F

2) Organizational development is one of the main areas of work for I/O psychologists. T-or-F

3) The AGCT was used to classify army recruits during WWII. T-or-F

4) The Family and Medical Leave Act allows for 12 weeks of paid leave for the birth of a child. T-or-F

5) A CIO is often the head of the IT department. T-or-F

Sample short-answer questions:

1) Identify and describe the six fields of I/O psychology.

2) Describe the main contributions of each of the founding fathers of I/O psychology: Walter Dill Scott, Frederick Taylor and Hugo Munsterberg.

3) Describe the impact of both workforce trends and industry trends on I/O psychology.

Answer key to multiple-choice items	Answer key to true-false items
1) b	1) F
2) b	2) T
3) c	3) T
4) a	4) F
5) a	5) T
6) b	
7) a	
8) b	
9) d	
10) a	

Chapter 2: Outline

Research

Generalizability

Three goals of science: describe, predict & explain

Five steps in the Empirical Research Process

1) Statement of the problem

Theory

Inductive v. deductive method

2) Design of the research study

Research design

Internal v. external validity

Naturalness

Degree of Control

Primary Research Methods

Laboratory experiment

Quasi-experiment

Questionnaire

16

Observation

Secondary Research Methods

Meta-analysis

Level of analysis

Qualitative research

Ethnography

3) Measurement of Variables

Quantitative v. Categorical Variables

Independent Variables

Dependent Variables

Predictor Variables

Criterion Variables

4) Analysis of Data: Descriptive statistics

Frequency distribution

Normal distribution (bell curve)

Negatively skewed distribution

Positively skewed distribution

Measures of Central Tendency

Mean

Median

Mode

Measures of Variability

> Range

> Standard deviation

Correlation

> Symbol for correlation

> Range of correlation

> Positive correlation

> Negative correlation

> Size of correlation

5) Conclusions from Research

> Value of a single study

> Generalizability

> Research as a cumulative process

Ethical Problems in Research

> APA Code of Ethics (2002)

> 1) Right to informed consent

> 2) Right to privacy

> 3) Right to confidentiality

> 4) Right to protection from deception

> 5) Right to debriefing

Research in Industry

    Organizational problems

    Use of results

    Motives for conducting research

    Actionable knowledge

<u>Concept Charts for Chapter 2</u>

Empirical Research Process

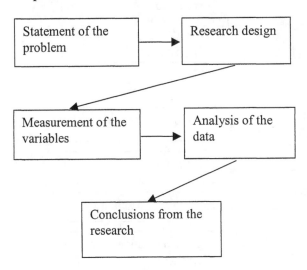

Descriptive Statistics

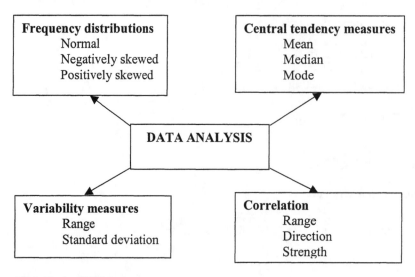

APA Code of Ethics

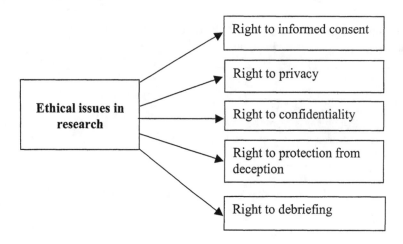

1) http://www.bls.gov/

This web site deals with statistics that I/O psychologists might be interested in. This site is run by the Bureau of Labor Statistics. It has numerous statistics relevant to the labor force as well as access to a variety of surveys.

2) http://members.aol.com/johnp71/javastat.html

This is a web page that connects you to other web pages that can allow you to perform various statistics, including those mentioned in this chapter.

3) http://www.pollingreport.com/Contents.htm

This web site reports the results of numerous public opinion polls, some of which deal with American business.

4) http://www.icpsr.umich.edu:8080/GSS/homepage.htm

This web site is the home page for the General Social Science Survey database. You can analyze data from the GSS surveys over the past 20 years or so.

5) http://www.apa.org/ethics/

This web site allows you access to APA's code of ethics revised as of 2002.

Exercise 2-1: Research Methods

DIRECTIONS: Following are examples of five studies related to industrial/ organizational psychology. After you read about research methods in your textbook, go through each of the five studies below and identify the research method, the independent and dependent variables, and consider how you might improve or expand upon the study that is described.

1. Available data still suggest that on average, women receive lower pay than men. A professor decided to design a program to train college women to

negotiate higher salaries. To assess the effectiveness of the program, 30 college women were randomly assigned to attend either a 12-hour salary negotiation skill training course or to be on a waiting list for the course. After the first group attended the training, both groups were tested on their negotiation skills by a trained individual (a graduate student) role-playing as an employer making a job offer. The individuals that had salary negotiation skill training negotiated a higher salary in the role-playing exercise.

Research method:

Independent (predictor) variable(s):

Dependent (criterion) variable(s):

Weaknesses of this study or the method:

Can you think of another study the professor might want to conduct to further understand this issue? Explain.

2. A researcher wants to understand to what extent variables such as financial difficulties, employment commitment (how much work means to a person), social support, and an individual's ability to structure his or her time and keep busy have an impact on mental and physical health during unemployment. In order to answer this question, 100 unemployed executives are asked to complete a questionnaire that asks questions about financial difficulties, employment commitment, social support, time structure, mental health, and physical health. Forty of the 100 questionnaires given out are returned.

    Research method:

    Independent (predictor) variable(s):

    Dependent (criterion) variable(s):

    Weaknesses of this study or the method:

    What other issues relevant to unemployment might the investigator want to study?

3. The Scandinavian Sweets Factory recently implemented shift work. The factory is now open 24 hours a day, and employees either work an early shift, a

late shift, or a night shift. The manager plans to compare each shift in six months to assess whether there are differences in the groups on productivity and turnover.

Research method:

Independent (predictor) variable(s):

Dependent (criterion) variable(s):

Weaknesses of this study or the method:

What recommendations would you make for further research?

4. A researcher wanted to examine whether a new machine would lead to increased productivity on an assembly line at Sam's Office Supply Factory. He randomly assigned ten workers to the new machine and ten workers to the old machine. The workers in the two groups were carefully matched in terms of their ability and experience. The researcher monitored the total number of products produced and the amount of product rejects on the two machines over a period of two weeks. Results showed the workers on the new machine had higher levels of productivity.

Research method:

Independent (predictor) variable(s):

Dependent (criterion) variable(s):

Weaknesses of this study or the method:

Can we now assume for certain that the new machine is better? Why or why not?

5. In a study of bias in work performance ratings, black and white undergraduate psychology students were assigned the task of providing work performance ratings for videotaped "employees" (really graduate students who were just pretending to be employees) who differed in terms of their race (black or white). Level of work performance was held constant on the videotape. Results showed that white raters tended to give slightly higher work performance ratings to the white employees on the videotape. Black raters, on

23

the other hand, tended to give slightly higher work performance ratings to the black employees on the videotape.

Research method:

Independent (predictor) variable(s):

Dependent (criterion) variable(s):

Weaknesses of this study or the method:

Why might it be difficult to study race bias in work performance ratings in a real organizational setting? What variables would you lose control over?

Exercise 2-2: Analysis of Data

You have been hired to conduct a job satisfaction survey for a local gift shop that has 15 employees. You have given the 15 employees a job satisfaction survey, and you have calculated a job satisfaction score for each person. Total scores can range from 0 (very low job satisfaction) to 40 (very high job satisfaction).

The norms for this job satisfaction survey suggest that individuals that score less than 20 on this survey are dissatisfied with their jobs. Following are the scores for each of the 15 employees you surveyed.

Employee	Score
#01	40
#02	20
#03	8
#04	7
#05	10
#06	12
#07	38
#08	39
#09	10
#10	12
#11	15
#12	19

#13	21
#14	11
#15	18

$$\Sigma =$$

DIRECTIONS: Read Chapter 2 of your book, then answer the following questions using this data.

(1) What is the average or mean job satisfaction score?

(2) What is the median job satisfaction score?

(3) What is the mode job satisfaction score?

(4) What is the range of observed scores?

(5) Draw a normal or bell-shaped distribution:

Draw a negatively skewed distribution:

Draw a positively skewed distribution here:

Which type of distribution best describes the job satisfaction data?

(6) Can you draw any conclusions from the data you have collected (e.g., Are the employees satisfied or dissatisfied? What might be happening in this organization? What follow-up work might you do?)

(7) Finally, let's say you decide to conduct a study on what variables are correlated with job satisfaction in this and other organizations.

(a) What variables would you guess might be positively correlated with job satisfaction?

(b) What variables might be negatively correlated with job satisfaction?

25

Exercise 2-3: Research Summary

This assignment involves writing a research summary. You will find a <u>research</u> article in a journal in the library. Then, you will write a short paper about the article. This assignment will help you to:
1) understand research methods used to study industrial psychology
2) become acquainted with research journals in psychology and business
3) improve your writing skills
4) learn more about a topic related to the course

Instructions: Find a <u>research</u> article (not a literature review) on a topic related to industrial/ organizational psychology for the summary. Write a 4-5 page double-spaced typed paper about the research article. Include the following information:
1) Purpose of the study
2) Methodology (e.g., subjects, measures used)
3) Main findings of study
4) Strengths and weaknesses of study (e.g., What is your opinion of this research? Does it interest you? Was it well done? How could the study be improved?)

Type your name in the top right corner of the first page. Number each page. Type the <u>complete</u> reference of your article at the top of your report in APA style (follow the format of your book's references and you will be fine). Cover the required information in the order listed above (purpose, methodology, findings, strengths). Include a heading for each of these sections. Staple a copy of the research article to your report. Do not copy sentences word for word from the research articles; this is plagiarism. You are to summarize the article in your own words.

<u>Eligible Topics:</u> The article you find should be concerned with a topic related to industrial/ organizational psychology (e.g., job analysis, job evaluation, the validity of interviews, personality testing, honesty testing, training, performance appraisal, leadership, work motivation, job satisfaction, work-related stress). The article must report results of a study related to any of these topics. It should not be a review article. If you have questions about the appropriateness of a topic, ask your instructor.

<u>Finding an article:</u> You may want to use Psych Lit or PsychInfo (ask your librarian for help) and search for an article on a topic of interest to you. You may also look through recent issues of I/O and business research journals to find a topic

that is "eligible" for the summary. Recommended journals to look through include: Academy of Management Journal, Journal of Vocational Behavior, Journal of Applied Psychology, Journal of Organizational Behavior, and Personnel Psychology. Your instructor may suggest other journals. Some journal articles will be difficult to read and understand. You are not expected to be able to interpret complex statistical analyses and tables, but you should be able to summarize the article's main findings.

Self-Test for Chapter 2

Sample multiple-choice items:

1) If you decide to research employee behavior by conducting an experiment in your college's psychology laboratory, then your study will have problems with:

   a) control
   b) internal validity
   c) external validity
   d) causation

2) All of the following are primary research methods EXCEPT:

   a) ethnography
   b) questionnaires
   c) quasi-experiments
   d) observation

3) In a research project on gender differences in employee productivity. Sex would be a:

   a) dependent variable
   b) qualitative variable
   c) quantitative variable
   d) criterion variable

4) If a researcher quantitatively integrated the results of 40 studies on a given topic, then the research method most likely used was:

   a) an ethnographic study
   b) a quasi-experiment
   c) a meta-analysis
   d) a qualitative analysis

5) Based upon the following numbers (0,3,3,3,4,5,5,6,7); what is the median?

   a) 3
   b) 4
   c) 5
   d) 6

6) Based upon the following numbers (0,3,3,3,4,5,5,6,7); what is the mode?

   a) 3
   b) 4
   c) 5
   d) 6

7) Which set of numbers would create a positively skewed distribution?

   a) 0,1,2,3,4,5,6,7,8,9
   b) 0,2,3,6,7,8,8,9,9,9
   c) 1,3,4,4,5,5,5,6,6,8
   d) 0,0,0,1,1,2,2,3,6,7

8) If you believed that the more hours per week full-time students worked, the lower their GPA would be, then which correlation would you hope to find?

   a) +.05
   b) -.02
   c) +.78
   d) -.83

9) The APA code of ethics was created to:

   a) ensure psychology research meets certain technical standards
   b) create a list of objectives to evaluate the quality of research
   c) protect psychologists from retaliation from disgruntled subjects
   d) safeguard the rights of research subjects

10) Research in industry is characterized by:

    a) testing theories pertinent to the organization
    b) a considerable amount of control over organizational practices
    c) arising from organizational problems
    d) a lack of actionable knowledge

Sample true-false items:

1) The inductive method of science starts with data and culminates in theory. T-or-F

2) A study can have external validity without internal validity. T-or-F

3) If a researcher was exploring the relationship between employees' weight and absenteeism records, these two variables would be categorical. T-or-F

4) A correlation of -.66 is stronger than a correlation of +.17. T-or-F

5) According to the APA code of ethics, researchers must answer subjects' questions regarding the research after the study is over. T-or-F

Sample short-answer questions:

1) Identify the 5 steps of the empirical research process.

2) Differentiate among the three goals of science: description, explanation, and prediction.

3) What the strengths and limitation of meta-analysis as a research tool?

Answer key to multiple-choice items	Answer key to true-false items
1) c	1) T
2) a	2) F
3) b	3) F
4) c	4) T
5) b	5) T
6) a	
7) d	

29

8) d
9) d
10) c

Chapter 3: Outline

Criteria

Conceptual Criterion

Actual Criterion

Criterion Deficiency

Criterion Relevance

Criterion Contamination

Bias

Error

Job Analysis

Three Major Sources of Job Information

1) job incumbent

2) supervisor

3) job analyst

Subject matter expert (SME)

Job Analysis Procedures

Task

31

Position

Job

Job Family

Task-Oriented Procedures

Task statements

Functional Job Analysis

People, data, things

Worker-Oriented Procedures

KSAOs

Linkage Analysis

How to Collect Job Analysis Information

Interview

Direct observation

Structured questionnaires

Inductive v. deductive approaches to job analysis

Taxonomy

Position Analysis Questionnaire (PAQ)

O*NET

Managerial Job Analysis

The Professional and Managerial Position Questionnaire

The Personality-Related Position Requirements

Uses of Job Analysis Information

Personnel selection

Compensation levels

Training

Performance appraisal

Vocational counseling

Connection of Job Analysis to the Americans with Disabilities Act

Competency Modeling

Competency

Competency modeling v. traditional job analysis

Job Evaluation

External Equity

Wage Survey

Internal Equity

Methods of Job Evaluation

Compensable Factors

Four common compensable factors

Hay Plan

33

Job Performance Criteria

    Appropriate

    Stable

    Practical

Eight Major Job Performance Criteria

    Production

    Sales

    Tenure or turnover

    Absenteeism

    Accidents

    Theft

    Counterproductive work behavior

    Customer service behavior

        Intangibility

        Simultaneity

        Coproduction

Relationship Among Job Performance Criteria

Dynamic Performance Criteria

Expanding Our View of Criteria

    "Good soldier"

    Prosocial behavior

Concept Charts for Chapter 3

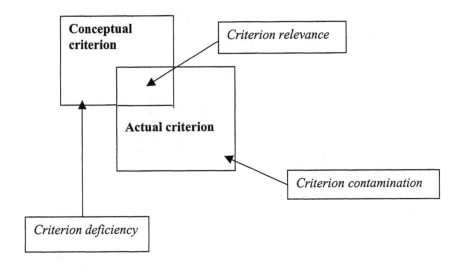

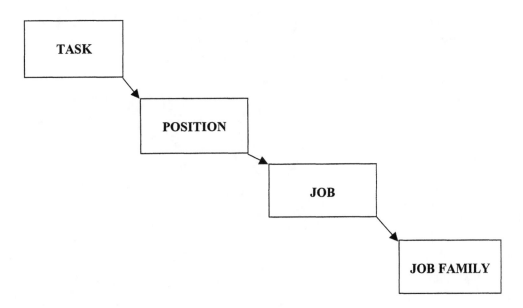

Three major sources of job analysis information

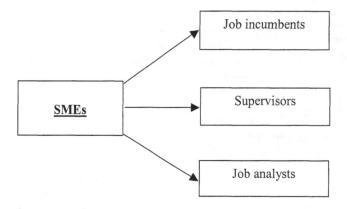

Job evaluation

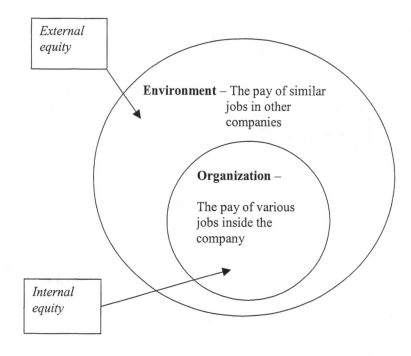

1) http://online.onetcenter.org/

This is the web site for O*NET.

2) http://www.wave.net/upg/immigration/dot_index.html

This web site provides information on the Dictionary of Occupational titles which preceded the O*NET.

3) http://harvey.psyc.vt.edu/JobAnalysis/resources.html

This web site provides information on job analysis.

4) http://search.eb.com/women/articles/comparable_worth.html

This chapter discusses fairness in pay. A related topic to fairness in pay is comparable worth, which focuses on gender differences in compensation. This web site provides an overview of this topic.

5) http://www.cba.uri.edu/Scholl/Notes/FES.htm

This web site provides much more detail on the factor evaluation system (an approach to job evaluation) than does the text.

Exercise 3-1: Pseudo Job Analysis Project

This exercise gives you the opportunity to conduct a mini or "pseudo" worker-oriented job analysis. You will summarize the results of your job analysis in a typed report that you will hand in to your instructor.

You will derive your job analytic information from one employee in a job of your choice using the interview method. You should choose to interview an employee who works full-time (or over 20 hours per week) in his or her job, and who has worked in his or her job for at least six months. The interview will most likely take one hour or more. You may want to tape record the interview. You should supplement the data derived from the interview with observational information (e.g., watch the person at work, visit the workplace, or look at samples of the person's work).

Your job analysis report should include the following five sections. Label sections 2, 3, 4, and 5 with a section heading. For example, you should have a section heading for the second part, labeled "Interviewee/Organization Information."

1. Cover sheet: Include a title (e.g., "Pseudo Job Analysis), your name, the date, the course number, and instructor's name.

2. Interviewee/Organization information: Include your subject's name (can make up or use real name), level of education, tenure, and rating of job satisfaction (1 = I hate my job to 7 = I love my job). Also include the individual's job title and what the organization does that the individual works for. Include information about how big or small the organization is, and how the individual's job fits in with other jobs in the organization.

3. O*NET Job Description: Go to the O*NET web site (see previous page) and look up the person's job title. You may have to experiment with different job titles to find a close match.

4. Knowledge, skill, and ability statements: Develop a list of knowledge, skills, and abilities (KSAs) needed to perform on the job (include 15-20 KSA statements). Do not just copy the information from the O*NET. Select the ones you believe are most relevant for the job. Write your KSAs clearly, be to the point, and do not be redundant. Sample KSA statements for the job of "medical technologist" have been included at the end of this exercise. After you have written your KSAs, you will need to meet with your subject one more time. First, have your subject review your KSA list

38

for accuracy (have you stated anything that is not correct?) and comprehensiveness (are all KSAs represented?). Then have your subject rate each KSA on "How often is this KSA used on the job?" (1 = rarely used, 2 = sometimes used, 3 = often used, 4 = very frequently used). This section of your report, when finished, should include your final list of KSAs and the rating your subject gave each KSA.

5. <u>What I learned from this project</u>: Write at least three paragraphs about what you learned from this project. Include information about what you learned from meeting with your subject a second time (e.g., were some of your KSAs stated incorrectly?). Include overall information about whether you found this project to be useful or difficult. Then include at least one paragraph explaining why job analysis is important to Industrial Psychology and how the information you collected could be used. How do you think this pseudo job analysis differs from a real job analysis?

<u>Other Tips:</u>

*   Prepare for your interview and arrive on time. You may want to start your interview by getting the information you need for section #2 of your paper. The main purpose of your interview, however, will be to get information about what KSAs are needed for a person to be a successful performer on the job.

*   Don't imply you are evaluating the <u>worth</u> of your subject's job. Don't say anything like "Is that all that you do?" You might offend the person you are interviewing.

*   Possible questions for your interview include: "What kinds of skills does a worker need to perform well in this job?", "Tell me what you do when you get to work each day," and "What skills or abilities does a good worker have that a poor worker doesn't for this job?" You can write notes as a person responds and form them into KSAs later. Clarify any occupational jargon a person might use.

*   When you write your KSAs, make sure they are not too specific or too broad. "Ability to write," for example, is too broad. Does that imply a person should be able to write novels, poems, songs, business reports, or what?

<u>Example KSA Statements for the Job of Medical Technologist</u>

Following is a <u>partial</u> list of the KSAs used in the job of medical technologist to give you an idea of how KSAs are written. Note that each KSA statement starts

39

with the word "Knowledge," "Skill," or "Ability." To the left of each of your KSA statements you can include your subject's rating (1 = rarely used, 2 = sometimes used, 3 = often used, 4 = very frequently used) of how often the KSA is used on the job. Be sure to provide the rating scale in your report to tell the reader what the ratings are referring to.

_____ 1. Knowledge of immunohematology, transfusion therapy, and phlebotomy.

_____ 2. Ability to conduct blood supply inventory and make judgements of present and predicted blood supply demands.

_____ 3. Ability to evaluate donor acceptability through an assessment of current health status and an interview concerning disease history.

_____ 4. Skill in blood collection process, including arm preparation, phlebotomy, and preparation of collection bags.

_____ 5. Skill to use standard laboratory instruments (microscope, centrifuge, platelet machine, and cell washer).

Exercise 3-2: The Good Professor?

Directions:

It is likely that at the end of this semester, in some or all of your courses, your instructors will pass out a student-teaching evaluation form (STE) for you to fill out. This form gives you an opportunity to give the professors and the college/university your opinions of various aspects of these courses with these instructors. STEs are often viewed as a reasonable measure (actual criterion) of being a good teacher (conceptual criterion), which is one major component of being a good professor.

In this exercise your instructor will break the class into small groups (probably 4 to 6 students). Your instructor will also pass out copies of the STE form used by your college/ university. Each group will examine these forms for criterion relevance, deficiency and contamination for the conceptual criterion of "good professor." In addition, each group will give their overall opinion of the STE as an actual criterion measure. Each group should designate a member to present to the class on the four areas listed below. The questions that follow will help your group as a guide through this evaluation.

Relevance:

- Which items do you think best capture what a good teacher should be?

- What characteristics of a good teacher is this form assessing?

- Which aspects of effective teaching does this STE hit upon?

Deficiency:

- What topics do you believe are missing in this form?

- Are there any aspects of being a good teacher that this form left out?

- Besides teaching, what are other aspects of being a good professor?

Contamination:

- Why do you think some students will rate this professor in this class higher or lower than other students?

- It is very likely that your professor will receive different ratings in other courses he/she teaches. What factors may account for these different ratings across courses for the same instructor that has little to do the quality of instruction?

- Similarly, across your campus STE ratings vary dramatically. Once again, can you think of any factors that may contribute to differences in ratings besides quality of instruction?

Overall opinion of the STE:

- After doing this evaluation, do you think highly of your college's STE? Why or why not?

- Is it a good actual criterion measure of the conceptual criterion of "good teacher?"

- Is it a good actual criterion measure of the conceptual criterion of "good professor?"

- Any recommendations how the form should be changed to be a better actual criterion measure of good teaching?

Exercise 3-3: Internal and External Equity

A relative of yours recently cashed in on some big earnings in the stock market. He now plans to open a chain of 10 new convenience store/gas stations in the Midwest. He plans to hire approximately 14 employees to work in each store. For example, for each store he thinks he will need the following employees:

1 store manager
2 assistant managers
8 cashiers
1 shelf stocker
1 part-time custodian
1 administrative assistant/bookkeeper

Your relative knows that you are currently taking an I/O psychology course. You and him get into a discussion, and several thought provoking issues come up. Read over the section on "job evaluation" in Chapter 3 of your textbook. Then answer the following questions, keeping the above example in mind.

QUESTIONS

1.   How should your relative go about determining what wages to pay each position?

2.   Are employees likely to be more concerned with internal equity or external equity issues? What might happen if employees feel there is not internal equity? What might happen if employees feel there is not external equity?

3.   What is a wage survey? Would a wage survey be useful in this instance?

4.   After talking to you, your relative considers doing a wage survey to assess what other convenience stores are paying their employees. Make a list of questions for your relative that he might want to ask other employers in the survey. For example, you would probably want more information than just "how much money are you paying your employees per year."

5.   Can you think of any reasons your relative should avoid paying his employees too much over what other employers are paying?

Self-Test for Chapter 3

Sample multiple-choice items:

1) In a research study on predicting successful sales clerks, the number of customers served per hour represents:

    a) the conceptual criterion
    b) the predictor criterion
    c) the actual criterion
    d) all of the above

2) A given company evaluates its production workers by recording the number of units produced per 8 hour shift. If a valuable part of this job is helping out coworkers when needed, then one could say units produced per shift has some degree of:

    a) criterion deficiency
    b) criterion contamination
    c) criterion error
    d) criterion bias

3) Which of the following is an example of a SME?

    a) PAQ   b) DOT
    c) CEO   d) Job analyst

4) The Functional Job Analysis is a good example of a:

    a) task-oriented procedure
    b) worker-oriented procedure
    c) competency model
    d) linkage analysis

5) A linkage analysis procedure examines:

   a) the relationship between jobs and positions in an organization
   b) the functions of a job and the KSAOs needed for the job
   c) the ideal manager in the context of job and departmental needs
   d) integrating the data collected from multiple sources of job information

6) The ___ is a resource that provides information on a wide variety of occupations, which also includes information on market conditions, compensation levels for various jobs and career assessment instruments.

   a) SME
   b) O*NET
   c) FJA
   d) PAQ

7) ___ is an alternative to traditional job analysis in that the organization identifies key attributes that can be generally applied across all jobs.

   a) Job evaluation
   b) Managerial analysis
   c) Competency modeling
   d) Worker-oriented procedures

8) Which of the following represents an employee's concerns over external equity?

   a) Employee believes coworkers are paid more than him/her.
   b) Employee believes supervisor is paid way too much in relation to his/her salary.
   c) Employee feels underpaid compared to peers at a comparable organization.
   d) Employee feels underpaid in relation to his/her performance review.

9) The dimension of customer service behavior that refers to the effect of the customer's behavior on the employee's behavior is called:

   a) contamination
   b) coproduction
   c) simultaneity
   d) intangibility

10) Being conscientious, helping others out, providing support to one's peers are all examples of:

a) dynamic criteria
b) competency modeling
c) compensable criteria
d) prosocial behavior

Sample true-false items:

1) Student grades would be an example of a conceptual criterion. T-or-F

2) A customer would be a common choice as a SME. T-or-F

3) Linkage analysis acts as a bridge between worker-oriented and task-oriented job analysis approaches. T-or-F

4) The results of competency modeling are usually applicable only to a specific job or a specific job family. T-or-F

5) Good job performance criteria should be practical and stable. T-or-F

Sample short-answer questions:

1) Briefly describe the three types of SMEs often used for collecting job analysis information.

2) How does job analysis differ from job evaluation?

3) Evaluate four of the eight major job performance criteria (production, sales, tenure, absenteeism, accidents, theft, counterproductive work behavior and customer service behavior) for criterion contamination and deficiency.

Answer key to multiple-choice items   **Answer key to true-false items**

1)	c	1)	F
2)	a	2)	F
3)	d	3)	T
4)	a	4)	F
5)	b	5)	T
6)	b		
7)	c		

8)   c
9)   b
10)   d

Chapter 4: Outline

Predictor

Assessing the quality of predictors

Psychometric criteria

Reliability

Test-Retest Reliability

Coefficient of stability

Equivalent-Form Reliability

Coefficient of equivalence

Internal-Consistency Reliability

Split-half reliability

Cronbach's alpha or Kuder-Richardson 20

Inter-rater reliability

Conspect reliability

Validity

Construct

Construct validity

47

Convergent validity coefficients

Divergent validity coefficients

Criterion-Related Validity

Concurrent criterion-related validity

Predictive criterion-related validity

Validity coefficient

Content Validity

Subject matter experts

Face Validity

Predictor development

Two dimensions to classify predictors

Psychological tests and inventories

Test v. inventory

History of psychological testing

Sir Francis Galton

Cattell

Ebbinghaus

Binet

Terman

IQ

Types of tests

       Speed versus Power Tests

       Individual versus Group Tests

       Paper-and-Pencil versus Performance Tests

Ethical standards in testing

       APA code of professional ethics

       Test user qualifications

       Invasion of privacy

       Confidentiality

       Retention of records

Sources of information about testing

       Mental Measurements Yearbook (MMY)

       Tests in Print VI

Test content

Intelligence tests

       "g"

       Sternberg's triarchic theory of intelligence

Mechanical aptitude tests

Sensory/Motor ability tests

Personality inventories

       Myers-Briggs Type Indicator

Big five theory of personality

"p-factor"

Integrity tests

Overt integrity tests

Personality-based measures

Physical abilities

Multiple-aptitude test batteries

Computerized adaptive testing

The value of testing

Situational judgment test

On-line computer testing

Interviews

Degree of structure

Situational interviews

Experience-based v. situational questions

"Illusion of validity"

Assessment centers

Sources of criterion contamination

Work samples

High-fidelity simulations

Situational exercises

>   Low-fidelity simulations

>   In-basket Exercise

>   Leaderless Group Discussion

Biographical information

>   Legal implications

Letters of recommendation

Drug testing

>   Screening test

>   Confirmation test

New or controversial methods of assessment

>   Polygraphy or Lie Detection

>   Graphology

>   Tests of Emotional Intelligence

Overview and evaluation of predictors

>   Validity

>   Fairness

>   Applicability

>   Cost

Three judgments of the job-related experience

Concept Charts for Chapter 4

Reliability

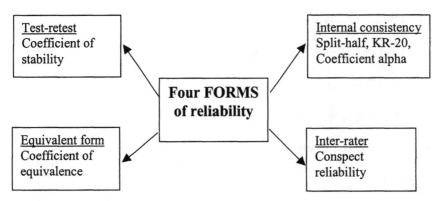

Test-retest
Coefficient of
stability

Internal consistency
Split-half, KR-20,
Coefficient alpha

**Four FORMS
of reliability**

Equivalent form
Coefficient of
equivalence

Inter-rater
Conspect
reliability

Validity

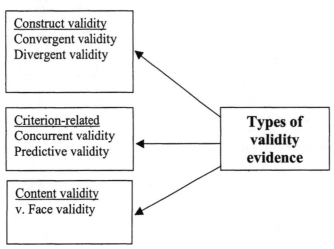

Construct validity
Convergent validity
Divergent validity

Criterion-related
Concurrent validity
Predictive validity

**Types of
validity
evidence**

Content validity
v. Face validity

Predictors

Intelligence tests	Mechanical aptitude tests	Sensory/motor ability tests
Personality inventories	Integrity tests	Physical ability tests
Multiple-aptitude test batteries	Computer adaptive testing	Interviews
Assessment centers	Work samples	Situational exercises
Biographical information	Letters of recommendation	Drug testing
Polygraphs	Graphology	Tests of emotional intelligence

Evaluation of predictors

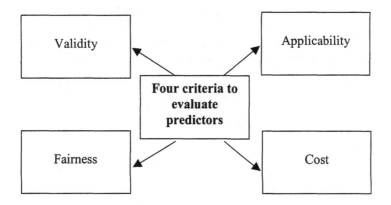

Web Sites for Chapter 4

1)   http://www.siop.org/_Principles/principlesdefault.htm

This web site provides access to the Principles for the Validation and Use of Personnel Selection Procedures. This site is run by SIOP.

2)   http://www4.law.cornell.edu/uscode/29/ch22.html

At this web site you will find information on the Employee Polygraph Protection Act.

3)   http://www.unl.edu/buros

This web site is run by the Buros Institute of Mental Measurements, which publishes the Mental Measurements Yearbook and Tests in Print. For a fee you could purchase reviews of numerous tests and inventories.

4)   http://www.iqtest.com/

At this web site you will find an IQ test you can take for fun. I have no idea of the reliability or validity of this test.

5)   http://www.fortune.com/fortune/quizzes/careers/eq_quiz.html

This web site is run by Fortune Magazine. This particular web page has an emotional intelligence test that you can take for fun.

Exercise 4-1: Assessing the Validity of a Clerical Selection Test

Assume for the purposes of this exercise that you are an I/O Psychologist. You have been hired by the XYZ Cola Company to develop and assess the validity of a clerical selection test. The intent of the clerical selection test will be to test applicants who want a job as a secretary.

The XYZ Cola Company currently has 2000 secretaries on payroll. The company has learned from experience that it is very important to have qualified individuals in their secretarial positions, and that top clerical employees seem to require less training time, produce higher quality work, and get higher performance ratings. Yet, they have never had a formal test to use for selecting new secretaries.

You complete a careful job analysis and find that there are four major components to the work done by the clerical workers at XYZ Cola Company. These components are as follows:

1. Filing

2. Recording and Checking

3. Written Communication Skills

4. Typing

You develop four tests to assess these skills. For example, Figure 4-1 shows an example of an item from your "Written Communication Skills Test". You decide to calculate a total score for each person who takes your test by adding his or her four test scores together.

Figure 4-1: Sample item from Written Communication Skills Test

---

Directions: Following are several sentences. The underlined part of each sentence may contain an error in spelling, punctuation, or capitalization. If the underlined part of the sentence contains an error, then mark the box in front of the change that should be implemented for the sentence.

The Federal Express package should arrive at <u>3:00 pm Wenesday</u>.
☐ 3:00 pm Wenesday
☐ 3:00 p.m. Wenesday
☐ 3:00 p.m. Wednesday
☐ NO CHANGE NEEDED

Based on the information given on the previous page, please answer the following questions. Chapter 4 of your book will also help you answer the questions.

1.   What does face validity refer to? Is the item in Figure 4-1 <u>face valid</u>?

2.   What does <u>content validity</u> refer to? How might you determine whether the clerical test you have developed has sufficient content validity?

3.   Give an example of how you might assess the <u>concurrent criterion-related validity</u> of your clerical test. Please be as specific as possible.

4.   How would you assess the predictive criterion-related validity of your clerical test? Please be as specific as possible.

5.   What would be an acceptable validity coefficient for your predictive criterion-related validity study in #4? ($r = ?$)

6.   How might you assess the <u>convergent</u> validity of your clerical selection test?

7.   Finally, how might you assess the <u>divergent</u> validity of your clerical selection test?

Exercise 4-2: Exploring the Situational Interview

Introduction:

Many employers are now using a type of structured interview known as the situational interview. In a situational interview, applicants are asked predetermined questions that require them to respond to what they would do in a hypothetical situation related to the job of interest. The hypothetical situation usually involves some kind of dilemma or choice of responses. For example, in the J. of Applied Psych. (vol. 72), Weekly and Gier (1987) provide the following situational interview question for a sales position:

A customer comes into the store to pick up a watch he had left for repair. The repair was supposed to have been completed a week ago, but the watch is not yet back from the repair shop. The customer becomes very angry. How would you handle this situation? (page 485)

When the situational interview is used, the interviewer must ask every applicant the same list of questions in a standardized manner. A scoring key should also be available to score every applicant's answer. Weekly and Gier (1987) provide the following scoring key for the situational interview question listed above (e.g., see page 485 of their article). The response listed at the low end of the scale (1) is supposed to indicate a poor response to the question, whereas the response listed at the high end of the scale (5) is supposed to indicate a good response to the question.

1 = Tell the customer it isn't back yet and ask him or her to check back later.

2 =

3 = Apologize, tell the customer that you will check into the problem and call him or her back later.

4 =

5 = Put the customer at ease and call the repair shop while the customer waits.

57

Assignment:

This exercise requires you to write a situational interview question and to develop a scoring key to evaluate answers to your question. Then you must administer the question to two friends or classmates who have not seen your questions. Finally, assess their responses.

1. Write a situational interview question for the job of your choice. Remember that the question should pose a hypothetical situation that might happen on the job, then it should ask the applicant what he or she would do in that situation.

2. Now you have to come up with a way to score answers to your question. Develop a 5-point Likert scale to score responses. On the low end of the scale (1), write what you feel would be a poor answer to the question. On the high end of the scale (5), write what you feel would be a very good or optimal answer to the question. In the middle of the scale (3), write what you feel would be an average or mediocre answer to the question. You can, but you do not have to, provide sample answers for ratings 2 and 4.

3. Now administer the situational interview question to two different friends or classmates that have not seen it. Make sure to ask the question of each individual in a standardized manner. Make sure to pause without talking to allow the individual to think about his or her answer. You may restate the question if needed. Write down each individual's response, and then score the answers.

4. What are your impressions of the situational interview? Would you, as a job applicant, like to be asked these kinds of questions?

Exercise 4-3: The Leaderless Group Discussion

Introduction:

A situational exercise commonly used in assessment centers is called the Leaderless Group Discussion (LGD). A LGD involves a group discussion (among the *assessees*, or the individuals being evaluated) on a hypothetical situation.

Trained *assessors* (individuals who are evaluating the individuals in an assessment center) watch the group discussion carefully and rate the individuals on several dimensions, such as ability to communicate. Many of you will have the opportunity to participate in an assessment center one day. Today you will participate in a class demonstration of the Leaderless Group Discussion. Some of you will be assessees, some will be assessors.

Directions:

Your professor will send five volunteers to the hallway to read over the discussion problem below. These people will be the *assessees*. They will have five minutes to think of some comments to share about the problem presented below. They will then come back and have a discussion in chairs arranged in a circle in front of the class. The remainder of the class should read over the rating forms (these people will be the *assessors*). Your professor will assign two different assessees for each assessor to rate.

Discussion Problem:

The department of psychology at your college/university has been asked by the president of your college/university to evaluate the undergraduate psychology program's <u>effectiveness</u>. You are a member of a committee that was quickly formed to come up with a proposal for the president about this issue. Your committee meets in five minutes. When you meet, your group should brainstorm and discuss the following:

(1)   What does "program effectiveness" mean?

(2)   What are some ways you could evaluate the program's effectiveness? Are these methods feasible? What are their advantages and disadvantages?

When your committee meets, you will have only 20 minutes to come to a consensus on 3-5 proposed methods to evaluate the psychology program. Be specific. If you cannot come to a consensus, you may propose another meeting be held to discuss this further.

For Assessors: Rating Form for Leaderless Group Discussion

Please rate your two assigned assessees on the following dimensions on this scale:

1	2	3	4	5
extremely weak		average		exceptional

	Assessee #	Assessee #
1. Participation: Example: Individual was enthusiastic and made strong contributions to the discussion.	_____	_____
2. Oral communication: Example: Individual used proper grammar and vocabulary and expressed thoughts clearly.	_____	_____
3. Creativity: Example: Individual tried to brainstorm different possibilities to evaluate the program, or was able to think of several advantages or disadvantages.	_____	_____
4. Leadership: Example: Individual made sure the group was making progress, tried to get others involved, or demonstrated other leadership behaviors in the discussion.	_____	_____
5. Listening skills: Example: Individual seemed to actively listen to the other individuals in the group, clarifying their points when necessary.	_____	_____
6. Decision making: Example: Individual demonstrated a strong ability to make sound judgments and decisions.	_____	_____
Total Score:	_____	_____

60

Sample multiple-choice items:

1) A company has a test that is very good at predicting success as salespersons for the company. Since the company is a very attractive place to work, applicants repeatedly try to land a job at this company. The company is concerned about applicants taking the same test over and over so the I/O psychologist on staff devises alternate forms of the test. The most critical type of reliability for this instrument is:

   a) convergent
   b) concurrent
   c) equivalent-form
   d) test-retest

2) Based upon the scenario described in the above question, the type of validity evidence found for the original version of the test is:

   a) content
   b) criterion-related
   c) conspect
   d) convergent

3) Which of the following statement is true?

   a) A test can be valid without being reliable
   b) A test can be reliable without being valid
   c) A test can be neither reliable nor valid
   d) Both "b" and "c"

4) ___ validity refers to the impressions by the test taker of the relevance of the test content.

   a) Face   b) Content
   c) Construct   d) Convergent

5) This American psychologist developed the concept of IQ:

   a) Terman   b) Galton
   c) Cattell   d) Binet

6) The "big five" theory examines:

   a) five types of intelligence
   b) five types of personalities
   c) five types of physical/motor skills
   d) five types of mechanical aptitudes

7) One approach to interviewing is to greet the applicant and "go with the flow" and see where you end up. This method often results in different interview questions across applicants for the same position. This approach would be considered:

   a) situational
   b) behavioral
   c) unstructured
   d) low-fidelity

8) Which of the following predictors is widely regarded as having low validity in employee selection?

   a) employment interview
   b) situational exercises
   c) work samples
   d) letters of recommendation

9) Motivating oneself, managing one's feelings, and handling relationships are parts of:

   a) emotional intelligence
   b) the big five theory
   c) assessment center components
   d) the triarchic theory of intelligence

10) When selecting a predictor which of the following criteria should be used:

   a) fairness
   b) applicability
   c) cost
   d) all of the above

Sample true-false items:

1) Split-half and KR-20 are both types of internal consistency reliability. T-or-F

2) Subject matter experts are critical in obtaining content validity evidence. T-or-F

3) The terms test and inventory are basically synonymous. T-or-F

4) The Myers-Briggs Type indicator is a well known cognitive ability test. T-or-F

5) An example of a high-fidelity simulation would be a work sample test. T-or-F

Sample short-answer questions:

1) Differentiate among the four types of reliability (test-retest, equivalent-form, internal consistency, and inter-rater) as well as the three types of validity evidence (construct, criterion-related and content).

2) Briefly discuss the major ethical issues in testing.

3) What is the key difference between high-fidelity and low-fidelity simulations? When would you use one over the other?

Answer key to the multiple-choice items	Answer key to true-false
items	**items**
1) c	1) T
2) b	2) T
3) d	3) F
4) a	4) F
5) a	5) T
6) b	
7) c	
8) d	
9) a	
10) d	

Chapter 5: Study Guide

PERSONNEL DECISIONS

Chapter 5: Outline

The Social Context for Personnel Decisions

Nepotism

Universalist cultures v. particularist cultures

The Legal Context for Personnel Decisions

Civil Rights Act of 1964

Title VII

Protected groups: race, gender, religion, color, and national origin

Age Discrimination in Employment Act of 1967

Americans with Disabilities Act (ADA)

Disability

Major life activity

Reasonable accommodation

Undue burden or hardship

Adverse Impact

Disparate impact

Disparate treatment

4/5ths rule

Equal Employment Opportunity Commission

Uniform Guidelines on Employee Selection Procedures

Major Court Cases

Griggs v. Duke Power Company

"Grigg's burden"

Albemarle v. Moody

"Deference of law"

Bakke v. University of California

"Reverse discrimination"?

Watson v. Fort Worth Bank & Trust

Wards Cove Packing Company v. Antonio

Societal Values and Employment Law

Civil Rights Act of 1991

Social justice in employment

Affirmative Action

Four goals of affirmative action

Passive interpretation

Preferential selection interpretation

Quota interpretation

2003 U.S. Supreme Court decisions – University of Michigan

Gratz v. Bollinger

Grutter v. Bollinger

Recruitment

Recruiting yield pyramid

"Social validity"

Bona Fide Occupational Qualification (BFOQ)

A Model of Personnel Selection

Principles for the Validation and Use of Personnel Selection Procedures

Regression Analysis

Regression Equation

Multiple Predictors

Multiple correlation (R)

Squared multiple correlation (R^2)

Multiple Regression Analysis

Multiple Regression Equation

Validity Generalization

"Law of small numbers"

A Model of Performance

Task performance

Citizenship performance

Adaptive performance

Selection

Predictor validity

Predictor cutoff

Selection ratio

Base rate

Selection Decisions

Predictor & criterion cutoffs

True Positives

True Negatives

False Negatives

False Positives

Determination of the Cutoff Score

Three guidelines in determining the cutoff score

Banding

Overview of Personnel Selection

Dual goals of personnel selection

General mental ability (g)

Test Utility and Organizational Efficiency

Utility analysis

Benchmarking

67

Placement and Classification

Placement

Classification

Vocational guidance strategy

Pure selection strategy

Successive selection strategy

Concept Charts for Chapter 5

Legality of personnel decisions

Key legislation:

Civil Rights Act (1964)
Age Discrimination in Employment
    Act (1967)
Americans w/ Disabilities Act (1990)
Civil Rights Act (1991)

Major court cases:

Griggs v. Duke power
Albemarle v. Moody
Bakke v. University of California
Watson v. Fort Worth Bank & Trust
Wards Cove Packing v. Antonio
2 University of Michigan decisions in 2003

Legal issues:

Discrimination
Adverse impact
Affirmative action
Social justice

Approaches to personnel selection

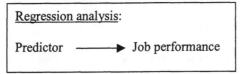

Regression analysis:

Predictor ——————▶ Job performance

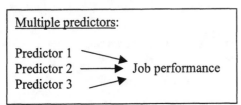

Multiple predictors:

Predictor 1
Predictor 2 ——————▶ Job performance
Predictor 3

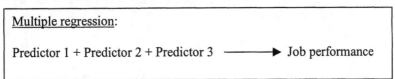

Multiple regression:

Predictor 1 + Predictor 2 + Predictor 3 ——————▶ Job performance

Selection decisions

J O B S U C C E S S	False Negatives Job success Failed predictor	True Positives Job success Passed predictor
	True Negatives Failed at job Failed predictor	False Positives Failed at job Passed predictor

SUCCESS ON PREDICTOR

1) http://www.jan.wvu.edu/links/adalinks.htm

    At this web site you will find the ADA document center.

2) http://www.monster.com

    This web site is the most well known Internet site for recruiting.

3) http://www.eeoc.gov/

    This web site is the EEOC home page. You can find a great deal of information pertaining to legal issues in selection.

4) http://www.supremecourtus.gov/

    This is the home page of the U.S. Supreme Court. As you know, this chapter mentions several important Supreme Court rulings. This web site allows you to search information pertaining to our country's highest judicial body.

5) http://www.siop.org/_Principles/principlesdefault.htm

    This web site provides access to the Principles for the Validation and Use of Personnel Selection Procedures. This site is run by SIOP.

Exercise 5-1: Decisions, Decisions, Decisions...

Real Estate World is trying to improve their selection process for hiring real estate agents. A successful real estate agent, according to the company, is one you can sell a minimum of 50 houses per year. The company believes that the key to successful real estate is perseverance. To test this hypothesis the company administers The Perseverance Assessment (TPA) to all 75 applicants with the proper real estate license. The company hires all of the applicants that scored higher than 3 on the TPA and gives all of them 1 year to see how they do. Given below are applicant scores on the TPA as well as how many houses each sold in the year. Answer the questions that follow.

TPA score	# houses sold in the year
10	78 67 65 59 55
9	79 61 61 61 58 56 56 50 48 47
8	69 65 64 63 59 56 50 50 50 49 45 44 42 41 31
7	72 66 56 55 54 53 52 51 51 51 50 43 42 33 21
6	62 61 60 59 52 49 48 45 44 43 42 40 40 29 20
5	55 52 51 50 50 43 41 33 29 18
4	57 49 40 27 22

Questions:

1. If 150 applicants scored 3 or lower on the TPA, what would be the **selection ratio**?

2. Assuming 50 houses sold per year is the criterion for success, what is the **base rate** for hiring real estate agents?

3. If the company decides to use 8 as the "Cutoff score" how many:

   - True positives? _____
   - False positives? _____
   - True negatives? _____
   - False negatives? _____

Criterion ⟶ Predictor ↓	"Bad hire"	"Good hire"
Pass (8 or higher on TPA)		
Fail (below 8 on TPA)		

4. What is the overall decision-making accuracy?

5. Would you recommend this test? Why or why not?

Exercise 5-2: Understanding Adverse Impact

Adverse impact refers to when a selection method leads to a disproportionate percentage of people of a given group to be hired compared to another group. Your book describes how to decide if adverse impact is occurring. This exercise will help you to assess your understanding of adverse impact.

Assume for this example that you are a human resources director of a large organization. You are interested in assessing whether a certain selection procedure is leading to adverse impact among minorities. With this information in mind, please answer the following questions.

1. To assess the adverse impact of the selection procedure, you need to know the selection ratio for minorities and nonminorities. What information would you need to calculate the selection ratio (a) for minorities and (b) for nonminorities?

2. Adverse impact is determined by the 4/5ths rule. Explain this rule.

3. You have collected the following data for the selection procedure you are interested in. In 2004, 300 nonminorities and 40 minorities applied for a job with your organization. Using your selection procedure, 60 nonminorities and 6 minorities were selected. Based on this information, is there evidence of adverse impact? Write your calculations and reasoning below.

4. If adverse impact is found to exist, what should the employer do?

Exercise 5-3: Hooters & What Is a BFOQ?

In Chapter 5 of your textbook, Field Note 1 discusses how a dentist who was looking for a partner could justify looking for a left-handed individual to join his practice, and thus not even consider hiring a right-handed dentist. Because the dentist was left-handed, and all of his instruments were left-handed, it was necessary for him to find a left-handed partner.

In Industrial Psychology, we call particular qualifications (such as left-handedness) that are enforced in hiring because they are reasonably necessary to the success of a business or enterprise "BFOQ's", or Bona Fide Occupational Qualifications. Another example of a BFOQ would be limiting your selection of a star for a documentary about Korea to an individual who is Korean. Although it is illegal to hire on the basis of race, being Korean may be a BFOQ when hiring for a documentary about Korea.

Following is an interesting article about a popular restaurant chain called "Hooters." At the time of this article, this case was far from being resolved. This case has now been settled. Your instructor will inform you how this matter was resolved after you complete this exercise. Read the newspaper article and answer the questions following the article.

EEOC call for male waiters is a drag, Hooters claims
By Bill Leonard (HRNews, December, 1995, Volume 14 (12), pp. 1-2) [1]

Hooters may be a restaurant where men go to play, but it's definitely not a place where they can go to work. At least that's what the Equal Employment Opportunity Commission (EEOC) claims.

The commission's complaints of sexual bias against the Atlanta-based restaurant chain have angered both the company's management and its famous "Hooter Girls" waitresses. Last month, Hooters went public with its fight against EEOC efforts to force it to hire male bartenders and waiters.

About 100 Hooters employees demonstrated along Pennsylvania Ave. in Washington, D.C. The women, clad in orange jumpsuits, carried posters and placards with slogans such as: "Men as Hooter Guys: What a Drag" and "EEOC, I like my job, let me keep it."

The restaurant chain also ran full-page ads in The Washington Post and USA Today picturing a mustachioed man dressed in the Hooter's girl uniform of form-fitting tank top (with falsies) and orange running shorts. Headlines said: "What's Wrong With This Picture?" and "The Latest from the Folks Who Brought You the $435 Hammer."

Hooters management says it is prepared to spend up to $1 million to kindle grassroots support for its fight against the EEOC. The company planned more rallies in Dallas, Atlanta, Tampa and Miami.

The EEOC dispute with Hooters began in 1991 when it brought charges of sexual bias against the restaurant chain, which has 170 restaurants nationwide. The EEOC identified approximately 1,400 male applicants who had been turned down by the chain for jobs as bartenders, hosts and waiters.

The commission proposed a five-year conciliation agreement that Hooters management rejected. The proposed agreement would:

* *Open job categories of waiters, bartenders and hosts to men.*

- Provide $10 million in back pay to the 1,400 men who had been previously turned down for the jobs.
- Develop an awareness and sensitivity training program.

Hooters management argues that its employment policy is necessary to maintain the restaurants' image and that the sex restrictions are "bona fide occupational qualifications" under Title VII of the Civil Rights Act.

"Hooters guys just don't make sense," said Hooters Marketing Vice President Mike McNeil at a press conference before the demonstration in Washington. "This doesn't make legal sense, this doesn't make economic sense, and– in light of the 100,000 case backlog at the EEOC– this doesn't make moral sense."

McNeil and other Hooters managers have likened their case to Chinese restaurants that hire only Chinese waiters or French restaurants that will hire only French staff. "There is only one restaurant where you can go and see a Hooters girl," he said.

The EEOC, however, has continued to dispute Hooters' position, and negotiations between the commission and the restaurant chain broke down in November. Hooters management then decided to go public with its campaign to thwart the EEOC proposal. In a Nov. 21 statement, the EEOC declined to debate the issue publicly but said, "We fail to understand what Hooters is seeking to accomplish through this expensive, well-orchestrated campaign other than to intimidate a federal law enforcement agency and, more importantly, individuals whose rights may have been illegally violated." The statement noted that some men filed a private class-action lawsuit last December in U.S. District Court in Chicago alleging discriminatory hiring practices by Hooters.

"At first glance, Hooters' defense does appear to be a pretty strong one," said Jack
 Raisner, a business law professor at St. John's University in New York. "But when you start to examine what a court will really focus on, whether the hiring policy is justified by bona fide occupational qualifications (BFOQ), their position may weaken some."

Raisner said Hooters has to prove that its business is based upon men coming to see the Hooters girls. It's easy to support a female-only BFOQ when hiring women as dancers or models, but the issue of women-only as restaurant servers enters a gray area, he said.

"Hooters would have to show that its business would be irreparably harmed if they hired male waiters," Raisner said. "And that could be tough to prove."

The restaurant chain claims that it does hire men for management positions, cooks and kitchen help.

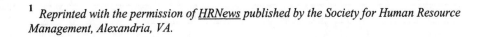

[1] *Reprinted with the permission of HRNews published by the Society for Human Resource Management, Alexandria, VA.*

Exercise 5-3 Questions

1.　Summarize the position of the EEOC:

2.　Summarize the position of Hooters:

3.　Do you think that being female is a justifiable BFOQ for Hooters' waitresses? Why or why not?

Sample multiple-choice items:

1) Based on the Civil Rights Act of 1964 which of the following would be illegal?

   a) Not hiring someone because they are too old
   b) Not promoting someone because he is Jewish
   c) Not considering someone for a job because they are in a wheelchair
   d) All of the above would be violations of the Civil Rights Act of 1964

2) To land a job in the warehouse, a company makes female applicants lift a 50-pound package to assess their strength to perform the job. The company does not make male applicants lift this package. This would be an example of a:

   a) disparate treatment   b) BFOQ
   c) disparate impact   d) social validity

3) According to the 4/5ths rule, if 6 males were hired out of 20 male applicants and 2 females were hired out of 10 female applicants, then:

   a) adverse impact exists
   b) adverse impact does not exist
   c) more information is required to assess adverse impact

4) In which major court case did the Supreme Court rule that discrimination based on any race, even if the plaintiff is white, is still discrimination?

   a) Watson v. Fort Worth Bank   b) Bakke v. University of California
   c) Albemarle v. Moody   d) Wards Cove Packing Co. v.
   Antonio

5) In the hiring process a company identifies the top three applicants for any open position. The company assumes that any of the top three would be more than qualified to fulfill the job demands. In accordance with the company's affirmative action plan, if any of the three belong to a minority, the minority applicant is offered the job. If none of the three are minorities, then the company randomly selects one of the top choices. This scenario is an example of a ___ interpretation of affirmative action.

   a) passive   b) preferential treatment
   c) quota   d) racially-biased

6) A graduate school has created the following multiple regression equation to predict graduate school GPA: $Y' = 1 + .60X_{maj} + .25X_{ove}$. You apply to this graduate school and your GPA in your major is 3.0 and your overall GPA is 2.8. Your predicted graduate school GPA based on this formula would be:

a) 2.75
b) 3.10
c) 3.50
d) 3.80

7) If 90% of employees in a given job perform that job at or above the company's expectations, then 90% represents the:

a) selection ratio for the job
b) base rate for the job
c) banding cutoff
d) predictor cutoff

8) Bob is hired for a job and after a few months the company realizes that he is unable to perform the job demands. The decision to hire Bob is an example of a:

a) false positive
b) false negative
c) true negative
d) true positive

9) Utility analysis

a) emphasizes the stability of validity coefficients across jobs
b) emphasizes the stability of validity coefficients across organizations
c) emphasizes the dollar value of using valid selection devices for hiring
d) emphasizes the value of banding processes over traditional approaches

10) In a pure selection strategy for classification and placement, you would…

a) allow the employee to choose whatever career path she wanted
b) select applicants based upon random selection
c) allow people to move into positions along as they are minimally qualified
d) choose the best person for the opening based on company values

Sample true-false items:

1) Nepotism may be viewed very positively as a hiring practice in some cultures. T-or-F

2) Disparate impact refers to treating people differently based on protected characteristics. T-or-F

3) The Civil Rights Act of 1991 made it illegal to adjust predictor scores based upon protected characteristics. T-or-F

4) The U.S. Supreme Court ruled against the University of Michigan's law school for considering race in their admission practices. T-or-F

5) A selection ratio refers to the percentage of employees that are successful at their job. T-or-F

Sample short-answer questions:

The text highlights five changes in the new millennium that have a significant impact on personnel decisions. Describe these changes.

What is validity generalization? Why is it relevant to this chapter?

Differentiate among true positives, true negatives, false positives and false negatives.

Answer key to the multiple-choice items	**Answer key to true-false items**
1) b	1) T
2) a	2) F
3) a	3) T
4) b	4) F
5) b	5) F
6) c	
7) b	
8) a	
9) c	
10) d	

Chapter 6: Outline

Skill enhancement

Director of training to chief learning officer

Learning

Three phases of skill acquisition

Declarative knowledge

Knowledge compilation

Procedural knowledge

Three major classes of abilities

General intellectual ability

Perceptual speed abilities

Psychomotor abilities

Three characteristics of experts

Proceduralization

Automaticity

Mental models

Meta-cognition

79

Self-efficacy

The pre-training environment

Assessing training needs

    Organizational analysis

    Task analysis

        Task statements

        Task clusters

        KSA analysis

        KSA- task links

        Physical fidelity

        Psychological fidelity

    Person analysis

Methods and techniques of training

Computer-based training

    Programmed instruction

    Intelligent tutoring systems

    Interactive multimedia

    Virtual reality

        Telepresence

Non-computer based training

    Business games

80

Roleplaying

Behavior modeling

Management development issues

Management development

Career velocity

Derailment

Glass ceiling

Cultural diversity training

Melting pot conception

Multiculturalism conception

Attitude change programs

Behavior change programs

Training for work assignments in foreign countries

Four key abilities for overseas assignments

Sexual harassment training

Equal Employment Opportunity Commission

Quid pro quo harassment

Hostile environment harassment

Three models used to explain sexual harassment

Natural/biological model

Organizational model

Sociocultural model

Mentoring

Mentors

Four states of the mentor relationship

Initiation phase

Protégé phase

Breakup phase

Lasting-friendship phase

Three-factor model of mentoring relationships

Frequency

Scope

Strength of influence

Two major dimensions to the mentoring relationship

Psychosocial

Task-related

Three types of peers

Information peer

Collegial peer

Special peer

Executive coaching

Three phases to executive coaching

Posttraining environment

    Transfer of training

    Generalization

    Maintenance

    Relapse-prevention training

Evaluation criteria of training programs

    Reaction criteria

    Learning criteria

    Behavioral criteria

    Results criteria

    Internal v. external criteria

    Four dimensions of training validity

        Training validity

        Transfer validity

        Intraorganizational validity

        Interorganizational validity

Concept Charts for Chapter 6

Organizational learning

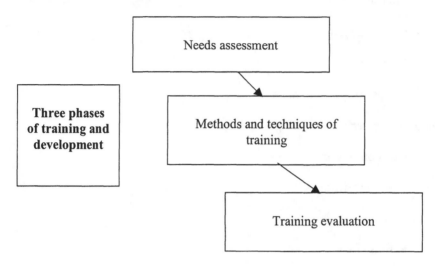

Three phases of training and development

Needs assessment

Methods and techniques of training

Training evaluation

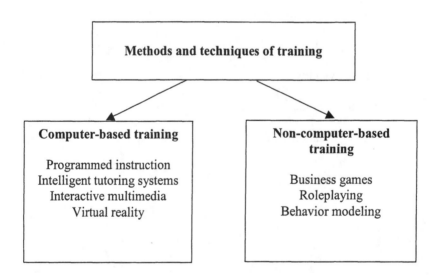

Methods and techniques of training

Computer-based training

Programmed instruction
Intelligent tutoring systems
Interactive multimedia
Virtual reality

Non-computer-based training

Business games
Roleplaying
Behavior modeling

Task analysis

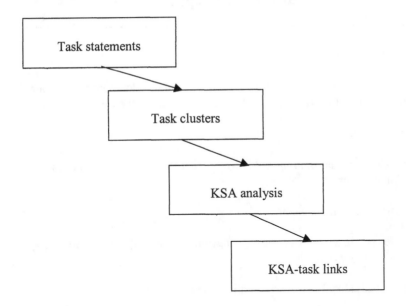

Evaluation criteria of training programs

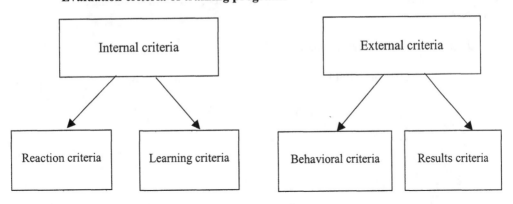

1)	http://www.astd.org/

The main professional association for training and development professional is the American Society for Training and Development. This is their web site.

2)	http://www.tcm.com/trdev/t2.html

This web site is the Training and Development Resource Page. It has tons of links to training resources.

3)	http://www.trainingmag.com/

This web site links you to Training Magazine, which will have numerous articles pertinent to this chapter.

4)	http://nt.media.hku.hk/interactivePatient/medicus.htm

This web site is an excellent example of a computer-based training program. It allows you to collect information on a fictitious patient and ultimately make a diagnosis.

5)	http://www.coachingnetwork.org.uk/

At this web site you can find information on coaching and mentoring.

Exercise 6-1: Planning a Training Program

You are the Training Director for a large company that sells office equipment. You have developed a wide variety of training programs for this company, and there is a course catalog that is circulated each year for employees.

Recently, it has come to your attention that a training program on listening skills would be useful for managers in this company. Several managers have identified this as a skill that they need to work on. Numerous employees have also complained that their managers do not listen to them very well, but instead jump to give their own viewpoints. You therefore feel that there is sufficient evidence that a training program on listening skills should be added to your course catalog, and you are now in the process of planning the exact content and format of this training program.

Planning a training program involves a lot of thinking and coordination. This exercise will ask you to think through several components of the new training program. Please answer the five questions on the following pages.

For Your Information:

Personnel Decisions, Inc. (PDI), a large consulting firm based out of Minneapolis, has published a book titled Successful Manager's Handbook with many important tips for managers. The book can also be helpful to trainers planning training programs for managers.

A few of the tips available in PDI's handbook on listening skills include:

1. Avoid interrupting people and don't respond too quickly.
2. Reschedule conversations with subordinates if you don't have time to listen.
3. Ask questions when clarification may be needed.
4. Avoid doing other work while listening.
5. Pay attention to your subordinate's body language.
6. Use reflective statements to summarize your subordinate's message.
    7. Use eye contact while listening, nod, lean forward, smile if appropriate.

1. Your first step should be to state the objective(s) of the training program. It will be useful to include the objective(s) of the program in the training catalog to make it very clear to employees what the purpose of the program will be. Stating the objective(s) will also help you stay on target when designing and evaluating the training program. State 1 to 3 primary objectives of your training program. Take care to make your objective statement(s) as specific and clear as possible.

2. Next, review the training techniques/methods described in your textbook. Which training method(s) would you want to use for your listening skills training program? Describe what the content of your program would include given your choice of methods. What advantages/disadvantages do you see with the methods you have chosen?

3. How many participants are you going to allow into each training session? How long will your training session be? Will you need to include breaks?

4. How will you evaluate the effectiveness of this training program?

5. What other things must you think about when planning this training program? Make a list of other issues/details you must attend to or organize.

Exercise 6-2: Task Analysis Exercise

The first phase of training and development is to conduct a needs assessment. The first step in needs assessment is organizational analysis. After the organizational analysis is completed, the next step of a needs assessment is the task analysis, which is then followed by a person analysis. This exercise focuses on the task analysis step of needs assessment.

Step 1: Select a job of interest

Make sure you select a job you know something about.

Step 2: Development of task statements

Create at least 10 task statements for this job. Recall from the text that "the goal of task analysis is to understand the work performed by an employee, as well as how the work is conducted and its purpose (p. 302). This page also provides a couple of examples of good task statements.

Step 3: Development of task clusters

Sort your list of task statements into at least three task clusters that reflect common job requirements. Label each cluster.

Step 4: KSA analysis

Write down the knowledge, skills (behaviors enhanceable through training), and abilities (cognitive or physical attributes that are primarily genetically determined) that a person in your chosen job needs to be successful. Make sure you separate the K, S., and A in this part of the exercise. Each statement in this section should begin with either K, S, or A.

Step 5: KSA-task links

Take a look at your task clusters and your KSA analysis. In this step you need to link or connect which KSAs go with each task cluster.

Step 6: Training methods

Assuming the person analysis step of the needs assessment finds that employees in your chose job are deficient in each task cluster. Come up with a training approach for each task cluster, keeping in mind the KSAs for that cluster. Which training methods would you use to develop the KSAs needed for that cluster? Why?

Exercise 6-3: Training Evaluation

Should a company spend thousands of dollars a year on a training program without trying to assess the effectiveness of the program? Let's say you get a position following graduation with a company that asks you to evaluate whether or not a particular training program is worthwhile. Would you know where to start? This exercise will help you think through the different components of training evaluation.

Instructions: Read the following training evaluation problem, then carefully answer the questions that follow. Before beginning, you should be familiar with Kirkpatrick's (1976) four levels of criteria for evaluating training programs.

TRAINING EVALUATION PROBLEM

"Walstart" has recently designed a training program for their employees on crime prevention. Employees will attend a two-hour workshop designed to train them to watch for shoplifters. They will also be taught procedures that should be used when identifying a potential shoplifter. You are called in to help Walstart evaluate the effectiveness of their training program. You decide to evaluate the crime prevention training program with all four of Kirkpatrick's levels of criteria. You are now sitting down to brainstorm how you can best go about doing this.

Questions:

1. First, describe how and when you will assess <u>reaction criteria</u>. Write at least three questions you would use to assess this level of criteria.

2. Now describe how and when you will assess <u>learning criteria</u>. Give some examples of the type of questions you will use to assess this level of criteria.

3. Carefully describe how and when you will assess <u>behavioral criteria</u>.

4. Finally, how will you assess <u>results criteria</u>? What are some aspects of the training program that will have to be documented as expenses? What are some aspects of the training program to document that may result in economic gain?

Sample multiple-choice items:

1) One characteristic of being an expert is that in your area of expertise you can perform many tasks without much cognitive effort. This characteristic is referred to as:

   a) proceduralization
   b) knowledge compilation
   c) automaticity
   d) meta-cognition

2) In terms of skill acquisition for driving a car, the phase that involves learning the features of the car (e.g., where the ignition is) would be the _____ phase.

   a) procedural knowledge
   b) declarative knowledge
   c) knowledge-compilation
   d) data gathering

3) Organizational analysis, task analysis and person analysis are all components of:

   a) a needs assessment
   b) a training evaluation system
   c) typical cultural diversity training programs
   d) an apprentice training program

4) Playing a video game that simulates driving a car may be low in _____ fidelity but may be high in _____ fidelity.

   a) task; psychomotor
   b) psychological; psychomotor
   c) psychomotor; physical
   d) physical; psychological

5) ___ occurs when a manager fails to live up to the expectations the company has had for him.

   a) Career velocity   b) Glass ceiling
   c) Fidelity   d) Derailment

6) One approach to managing a diverse workforce is to ignore cultural differences and treat all employees according to the same rules. This color-blind perspective is called:

   a) a derailment view
   b) a melting pot conception
   c) a sociocultural view
   d) a multiculturalism conception

7) If you believe sexual harassment is the result of status differences (superior-subordinate relationship) in companies, then you are adopting the ___ model of sexual harassment.

   a) organizational
   b) institutional
   c) bureaucratic
   d) hostile environment

8) Jason is an executive vice-president of the eastern division of company XYZ. He occasionally meets with Rachel, who is an assistant manager in the northern division of XYZ, to provide her with both job-related guidance and psychosocial support. Jason most likely is Rachel's:

   a) special peer
   b) executive coach
   c) mentor
   d) protégé

9) After the training program ends, the trainers ask the trainees what they thought of the program. Did they like it? Are they glad they came? This is an example of the ___ level of training evaluation.

   a) reaction   b) learning
   c) behavioral   d) results

10) A consulting firm advertising a training program they have developed that increased productivity by 20% at a well-known organization. The advertisement suggests that similar results will occur for your organization. This ad assumes high ___ validity.

a) training
b) transfer
c) intraorganizational
d) interorganizational

Sample true-false items:

1) The title "director of training and development" is commonly referred to today as the "Chief Information Officer." T-or-F

2) Your belief in your own ability to complete a task is referred to as self-efficacy. T-or-F

3) If a training program provided the trainee with text, video, animation and sound, it would be an interactive multimedia training approach. T-or-F

4) In mentoring there are typically three phases to the mentoring relationship. T-or-F

5) In evaluating whether or not a training program will work as well with the next group of employees, I am focusing on the intraorganizational validity of the training. T-or-F

Sample short-answer questions:

1) Differentiate among declarative knowledge, knowledge compilation, and procedural knowledge.

2) How are the three major classes of abilities (general intellectual, perceptual speed, and psychomotor) different? Provide an example of each.

3) What are the three phases to executive coaching?

Answer key to the multiple-choice items	Answer key to true-false

items

1) c
2) b

1) F
2) T

3) a   3) T
4) d   4) F
5) d   5) T
6) b
7) a
8) c
9) a
10) d

Chapter 7: Outline

Performance appraisal v. performance development

Performance management

Performance v. effectiveness

Four major uses of performance appraisal information

Enhance quality of organizational decisions

Enhance quality of individual decisions by employees

Can affect employees' views of and attachment to the organization

Provide a rational, legally defensible basis for personnel decisions

Using the results of performance appraisals

Personnel training

Wage and salary administration

Placement

Promotions

Discharge

Personnel Research

Performance appraisal and the law

Negligence

Defamation

Misrepresentation

Theory of person perception

Inputs

Processes

Outputs

Schemas

Sources of performance appraisal information

Objective production data

Personnel data

Rating errors

Halo error

Valid v. invalid halo

Leniency error

Positive v. negative leniency (severity error)

Central tendency error

Judgmental data

Graphic rating scales

Employee-comparison methods

Rank-order method

Paired-comparison method

Forced-distribution method

Behavioral checklists and scales

Critical incidents

Behaviorally anchored rating scales (BARS)

Behavioral-observation scales (BOS)

Rater training

Rating error focus

Frame-of-reference training

Rater motivation

Willingness v. capacity to rate

"Appraisal politics"

Contextual performance

Organizational citizenship behavior

Extra-role behavior

Self-assessments

Peer assessments

Peer nomination

Peer ratings

97

Peer rankings

360-degree feedback

Multi-source feedback

Three dimensions

People

Change

Structure

Differences between developmental & administrative uses

Feedback of appraisal information to employees

Performance appraisal interview

Credibility

Power

Concept Charts for Chapter 7

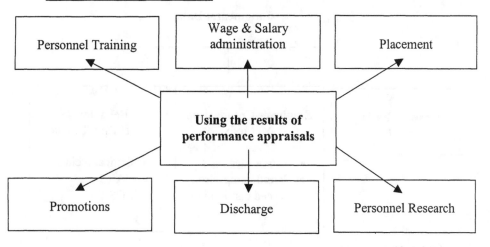

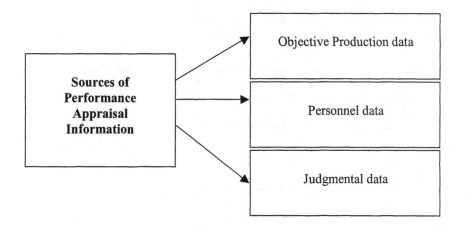

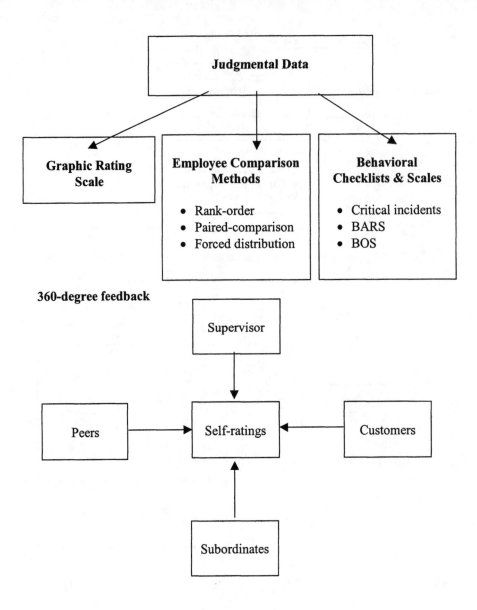

Web Sites for Chapter 7

1) http://www.zigonperf.com/

At this site performance appraisal resources are available.

2) http://www.360-degreefeedback.com/

This web site provides information on 360-degree feedback.

3) http://www.hr.ucdavis.edu/Forms/All/Perf_Eval

This web site provides the actual performance appraisal forms used at the University of California – Davis location.

4) http://iso9k1.home.att.net/pa/performance_appraisal.html

This web site also provides information of performance appraisal.

5) http://www.performance-appraisal.com/intro.htm

Here is one more web site that provides information on performance appraisal.

Exercise 7-1: Employee Comparison Methods

This exercise will help you become more familiar with the rank-order method and the paired-comparison method of performance appraisal. You will rank-order and conduct paired-comparisons for the last six professors you have had. To start, please make a list of the last six professors you have had. Do not include the instructor for this course.

Professor A (Name):   Professor D (Name):
Professor B (Name):   Professor E (Name):
Professor C (Name):   Professor F (Name):

Using the Rank-Order Method. Rank the professors you listed above from "most effective instructor" to "least effective instructor."

Using the Paired-Comparison Method: Keeping in mind the names of each professor, for each pair circle which professor you believe is more effective.

Professor A versus Professor B   Professor A versus Professor C

Professor A versus Professor D   Professor A versus Professor E

Professor A versus Professor F   Professor B versus Professor C

Professor B versus Professor D   Professor B versus Professor E

Professor B versus Professor F   Professor C versus Professor D

Professor C versus Professor E   Professor C versus Professor F

Professor D versus Professor E   Professor D versus Professor F

Professor E versus Professor F

Now count the number of times each professor was selected as the best.

A: _____   D: _____

B: _____   E: _____

C: _____   F: _____

Evaluating the Rank-Order and Paired-Comparison Methods: Did you find the same or different results when using these two different methods? What advantages and disadvantages do you see with each method?

Exercise 7-2: Let's Go to the BARS!

As the chapter indicates there are many approaches to developing performance appraisal forms. If you decide to assess employee performance using judgmental data, the most helpful approach for employee development is to use behaviorally anchored rating scales (BARS). This exercise will give you an idea how the BARS approach works.

For this exercise your instructor will divide the class into small groups. Once in your group complete the following steps:

a) Think about instances (behavioral events) in your college career that are reflective of either "highly effective" or "highly ineffective" teaching. Please do not use instances that have occurred in this course.

b) Designate a recorder before you start to share your experiences.

c) Go around the group and share these instances without indicating the instructor's identity.

d) After your group has identified approximately 10 critical incidents of "highly effective" or "highly ineffective" teaching, try to cluster your instances around common themes (e.g., student evaluation, presentation style, student involvement).

e) For each theme you created (no more than 3 or 4), devise a BARS for that theme with at least three levels (highly effective to acceptable to highly ineffective). Make sure each level describes in behavioral terms this component of teaching.

f) At the end of this activity each group will share their three or four BARS items that could be used to evaluate teaching at your college or university.

g) Your instructor may also want you to reflect on this approach to evaluating teachers compared to the student-teacher evaluations used at your college. Which system do you think is better from a student view? If you were an instructor which approach would you prefer? Justify your answers.

Exercise 7-3: How is Performance Evaluated at Your Organization

This exercise will give you the opportunity to find out more about performance appraisal in the "real world." You will be required to interview a human resources director or a manager that conducts performance appraisals of his or her employees. You will ask this individual questions that will help you to understand more about how his or her organization evaluates its employees.

Step 1: Visit an Organization

Identify a local organization that you wish to interview about their performance appraisal system. Call this organization and ask for a human resources director or for a manager. Explain that you would like to learn more about performance appraisal at their organization, and that you would like to schedule an appointment to meet with someone at their organization who conducts performance appraisals with his or her subordinates.

When you meet with an individual from this organization, ask several questions that will help you learn more about performance appraisal at that organization. Following are a few sample questions to get you started.

1. What is your job title? How many individuals do you supervise? What do they do? Do you conduct evaluations with all of them?

2. How often do you conduct performance reviews? In your opinion, is this often enough? Too often? About right?

3. Do you have a standard form that you use to evaluate the job performance of your subordinates? Can I see an example of this form? (If a sample copy is not available for you to review, ask what dimensions of job performance individuals are evaluated on and what type of scale is used.)

4. What do you like about conducting performance appraisals? What do you dislike? Do you see a need for improvement in the performance evaluation procedures or forms used at this organization? Do the employees like the procedures used?

Step 2: Summarize your Findings

Write a 2-page report detailing the information you gathered from your interview. Attach a copy of a performance appraisal form from the organization if they gave you one. Include the name of the individual you interviewed, his or her job title, and the name of the organization. Then, describe:

(a)   The performance appraisal procedures followed in the organization or job you focused on. (e.g., How often is performance appraised? Is there a standard performance appraisal form used to evaluate performance? How long is it, and what dimensions are included on it? What type of rating scale is used?)

(b)   Advantages and disadvantages of the performance appraisal process used at the organization that you can see or that the individual you interviewed pointed out.

(c)   Any additional comments and a brief summary of what you feel you learned from doing this exercise.

Other Tips:

- Prepare for your interview before your appointment and show up on time. Outline the questions you want to ask and be prepared to take notes. You may want to ask if you can use a tape recorder.

- You may decide to interview a manager or human resources professional at the organization you currently work for. The exercise will be most useful for you, however, if you are not already familiar with the performance appraisal system being used. If you are already familiar with the system at the organization you work for, it would be best to choose another organization.

- If you choose a large organization for this assignment, it will be useful to limit your discussion to performance appraisal of one particular job. For example, if you choose a hospital, you may want to limit your discussion to performance appraisal of the nurses at the hospital.

Sample multiple-choice items:

1) Performance appraisals are useful for all of the following reasons EXCEPT:

   a) Can improve the quality of organizational decisions
   b) Can help evaluate benefits provided by the employer
   c) Can improve the quality of employees' decisions regarding their career
   d) Can provide documentation in a lawsuit for wrongful discharge

2) Performance appraisals can be used for all of the following I/O psychology functions EXCEPT:

   a) promotions   b) recruiting
   c) personnel research   d) employee training

3) In a performance appraisal of Mary, her supervisor falsely includes comments that suggest Mary is lazy, uncooperative and slow-witted. Mary might sue the company based upon which legal concept?

   a) defamation   b) negligence
   c) procedural due process   d) prima facie
   discrimination

4) Brad's performance evaluation looks at two factors: accidents and absenteeism. This company relies upon which source of performance appraisal information?

   a) objective production data
   b) judgmental data
   c) personnel data
   d) deductive data

5) If your supervisor believes that you are very bright and based on this assessment, rates you incorrectly high on other traits (such as conscientiousness, initiative, etc.), then most likely he is committing which type of error?

   a) leniency error   b) central tendency error
   c) acquiesce error   d) halo error

6) In a performance appraisal system all employees are rated on a 1 to 10 scale in which 10 equals "excellent" and 1 equals "poor." This scale is used to rate employees on several dimensions including such aspects as: quality of work, quantity of work, and initiative. This system sounds like a:

a) graphic rating scale
b) BARS
c) BOS
d) rank-order scale

7) Which of the following would you most likely see in a BOS approach to performance appraisal?

a) Joe is better than John but not as good as Sue.
b) Lisa is rated a 5 ("excellent") on cooperation.
c) Samantha meets expectations 75% of the time.
d) Mike and Holly are poor performers.

8) Contextual performance refers to:

a) performance on essential job functions
b) performance that is subject to the rater's motivation and ability
c) performance in relation to one's peers
d) performance in areas not required but valuable to the company

9) In which approach do peers assess each other on several work-related dimensions?

a) peer ratings
b) peer rankings
c) peer nomination
d) both "a" and "b"

10) All of the following are true regarding performance appraisal interviews EXCEPT:

a) Typically supervisors are not anxious about the interview with their subordinate.
b) Subordinates are typically nervous going into this interview.
c) A typical objective of the interview is for future planning.
d) All of the above are true regarding performance appraisal interviews.

Sample true-false items:

1) Performance development is synonymous with performance management. T-or-F

2) If a company presents a false <u>positive</u> view of an employee's performance to a third party that may result in harm to that third party, then the company has legally exposed itself to a potential charge of misrepresentation. T-or-F

3) If a professor does not give out "A"s and "B"s in her course, a case may be made for the rating error known as "negative leniency." T-or-F

4) An example of a behavioral checklist is the forced comparison method. T-or-F

5) If multi-source feedback was used for developmental purposes only, the feedback should occur as often as compensation decisions are made at the company. T-or-F

Sample short-answer questions:

1) Discuss three ways in which the results of performance appraisal can be used for various I/O psychology functions.

2) Differentiate among the three sources of performance appraisal information: objective data, personnel data and judgmental data.

3) What is "appraisal politics?"

Answer key to the multiple-choice items	Answer key to true-false items
1) b	1) F
2) b	2) T
3) a	3) T
4) c	4) F
5) d	5) F
6) a	
7) c	
8) d	
9) d	
10) a	

Chapter 8: Outline

Three theories of organizations

    Organization

Classical theory

    Four basic components to any organization

        A system of differentiated activities

        People

        Cooperation toward a goal

        Authority

    Four major structural principles

        Functional principle

        Scalar principle

            Unity of command

        Line/staff principle

        Span-of-control principle

    Main contribution of classical theory

Neoclassical theory

Critique of the four major structural principles of classical theory

Functional principle

Scalar principle

Line/staff principle

Span-of-control principle

Main contribution of neoclassical theory

Systems theory

Five parts of an organization

Individuals

Formal organization

Small groups

Status and role

Physical setting

Main contribution of systems theory

Organizational structure

Structure

Coordinating mechanisms

Mutual adjustment

Direct supervision

Standardization of work processes

Standardization of work output

Standardization of skills and knowledge

Mintzberg's five basic parts of an organization

Operating core

Strategic apex

Middle line

Technostructure

Support staff

Centralization v. decentralization

Three reasons for decentralization

Reorganizing and downsizing

Reorganizing

Downsizing (reduction-in-force, rightsizing)

Components of social systems

Social system

Three informal components:

Roles

Five aspects of roles

Role episode

Role differentiation

Norms

    Four important properties of norms

    Three-step process for developing & communicating norms

Organizational Culture

    Culture

    Three layers of culture

        Observable artifacts

        Espoused values

        Basic assumptions

    ASA cycle

Global organizations

Western v. non-western values

Four key dimensions of value differences

    Leadership roles and expectations

    Individualism and groups

    Communications

    Decision-making and handling conflict

Hofstede's four main dimensions on cross-cultural differences

    Power distance

    Individualism-collectivism

    Masculinity-femininity

113

Three types of change

Self-initiated versus imposed change

Evolutionary versus revolutionary change

Additive versus subtractive change

Concept Charts for Chapter 8

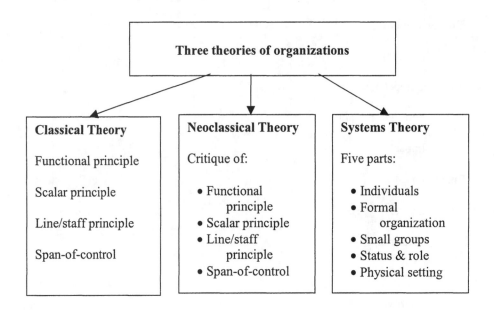

Three theories of organizations		
Classical Theory	**Neoclassical Theory**	**Systems Theory**
Functional principle	Critique of:	Five parts:
Scalar principle	• Functional principle	• Individuals
Line/staff principle	• Scalar principle	• Formal organization
Span-of-control	• Line/staff principle	• Small groups
	• Span-of-control	• Status & role
		• Physical setting

Mintzberg's Five Parts of an Organization

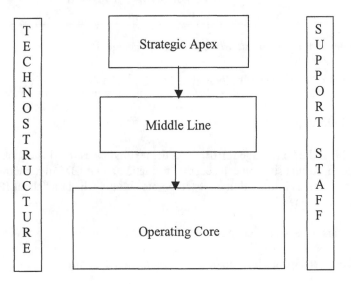

Six Sigma

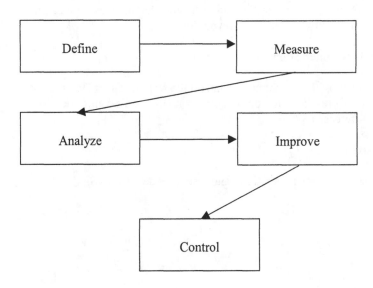

Web Sites for Chapter 8

1) http://www.dmsp.dauphine.fr/Management/Management.html

This web site is an on-line journal called M@n@gement, which provides numerous articles on organizational research topics discussed in this chapter.

2) http://www.ibm.com/

This is the home page for IBM. As the text indicates, IBM is a global organization. At this site you can access information about IBM in numerous other countries as well as information on its corporate culture. Click on "about IBM" and then click on "values."

3) http://mars.wnec.edu/~achelte/grad12outline.htm

This web site has information on organizational culture.

4) http://deming.eng.clemson.edu/pub/den/

This is the Deming Electronic Network web site. Deming was responsible for starting the Total Quality Management revolution.

5) http://geert-hofstede.international-business-center.com/

This web site provides much more detail on the work of Geert Hofstede. It allows you to obtain scores for numerous countries on Hofstede's four dimensions of cross-cultural differences.

6) http://www.isixsigma.com/

This web site has numerous articles and resources devoted to Six Sigma.

Chapter 8 begins with the three major schools of thought about organizations: Classical Theory, Neoclassical Theory, and Systems Theory. The chapter then moves on to Mintzberg's five basic parts of organization's structure. This exercise requires you to apply the main ideas from these theories to the following organization. Please read the following case study, then answer the questions following.

Snak Pak Attak Inc.[*] is the country's third leading producer of junk food. Some of its products are: Cauliflower Chips, Pimento Pretzels, Pepperoni Popcorn, and everybody's favorite Sardine Salsa Nacho Chips. To give you an idea of the company's influence in the U.S. junk food market, for the past three years the company has had sales exceeding 3 billion dollars and market shares ranging from 17% to 19%.

The company has not always been this successful. The company was founded by I. B. Leaveit in the early 1980s. I. B. took notice of the success of Ben & Jerry's creative approach to ice cream. He thought this strategy could work in the snack food industry. Of course, his products are much more unusual than anything by Ben & Jerry's. In 1982, he opened up a small factory in Iowa and began Snak Pak Attak. The company's motto is "Vegetable, Mineral, or Animal: Anything could be a snack food". It took a while for Snak Pak Attak products to catch on. By 1986, Sardine Salsa Nacho Chips became very trendy when Americans recognized the value of eating more fish. I. B. realized he had to expand his production facilities. In 1990, three newer and much larger production plants were opened in various locations across the U.S. In the early 1990s, Americans became concerned about reducing fat in their diet. The demand for Snak Pak Attak's Cauliflower Chips skyrocketed (only 2 grams of fat per serving). Further, Snak Pak Attak came out with a new healthful snack option, which had instant success: Brussel Sprout Baguettes. A thin crispy wafer with chunks of real brussel sprouts. Within the last year, Snak Pak Attak had added two more production facilities, doubled its sales staff, and has heavily automated its production line.

The company's organizational chart is in Figure 8-1. As you can see from the chart, I. B. is the CEO of the company. There are, however, a few aspects of the organization's design that are not evident from the chart. To begin with, under the vice-president of production operations there are 6 plant managers; one for each plant. There are 4 assistant plant managers for each plant manager. Further, each assistant plant manager is responsible for 10 foreman. Moreover, each foreman supervises 20 production workers. For the sales division, there are 5 regional sales directors: northeast, southeast, midwest, northwest, and southwest. Within each

117

region there are 6 area coordinators. Each area coordinator supervises 30 salespeople. Additionally, there are several positions that do not appear on the chart. There are clerical staff for each position from the foreman on up. Further, there is a considerable staff for each vice-president (e.g., human resource administrators, accountants, research scientists, marketing representatives). Security, custodians, mail clerks, and purchasing agents are also employed at each plant.

Job satisfaction at Snak Pak Attak is quite high, except for production workers. Production workers go through an extensive training program once they are hired. They are trained to do one highly specific job (functional specialization). Some of the production specialties are: bag fillers (fill package with exact amount of snack food), bag sealers (seal package), boxers, etc. It is quite common for production workers to become quite bored with their jobs in a relatively short time. The company did try to increase the production workers' job satisfaction by implementing an incentive system. The more units you produce, the larger your bonus will be. The program didn't work. Management failed to realize that production workers have an unwritten and unspoken code not to exceed the quota. The one production worker that did exceed the quota was "dealt with" discreetly by his co-workers. He surprisingly quit the week after he received his incentive bonus.

Overall, Snak Pak Attak is doing well in the fast food industry. The company has several plans for the next few years. One change the company is going to make is to take advantage of NAFTA (North American Free Trade Agreement) by expanding their distribution into Mexico and Canada. Further, the company is going to introduce two healthier snack foods to appeal to consumer demands (Cucumber Crackers & Possum Peanuts). Feel a little hungry?

*Please note that Snak Pak Attak is a fabricated organization. Any similarity to a real organization is purely coincidental and somewhat disturbing.

Questions:

(1) Classical Theory identified four main structural properties of organizations. Describe each of these properties as they apply to Snak Pak Attak.

    a) Functional principle

    b) Scalar principle

    c) Line/staff principle

    d) Span-of-control principle

(2) Neoclassical Theory attacked each of the four structural properties identified by Classical Theory. Critique your response to question #1 using Neoclassical arguments.

    a) Functional principle

    b) Scalar principle

    c) Line/staff principle

    d) Span-of-control principle

(3) Systems Approach views organizations as analogous to living organisms. Using Systems Theory concepts of stability, growth, and adaptability describe Snak Pak Attak.

(4) There are five basic parts to any organization according to Mintzberg. Apply each of these parts to this organization.

    a) operating core

    b) strategic apex

    c) middle line

    d) technostructure

    e) support staff

<u>Figure 8-1:</u> Organizational Chart

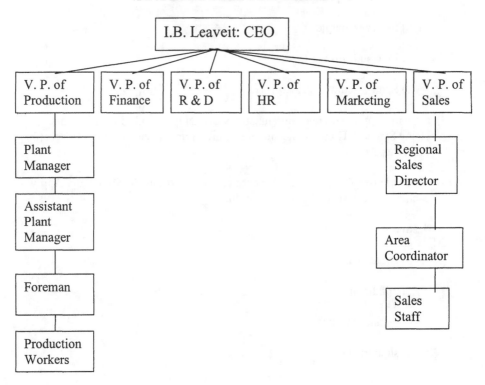

SNAK PAK ATTAK

Exercise 8-2: Examining Social Systems

The next part of Chapter 8 examines the three main components of social systems: roles, norms, and organizational culture. The text defines roles as "the expectations of others about appropriate behavior in a specific position", whereas norms are defined as "shared group expectations about appropriate behavior." Lastly, culture consists of "languages, values, attitudes, beliefs, and customs of an organization." As you can see these terms are quite similar. The way to differentiate among these terms is to determine the level of analysis. Roles focus on the *individual's position* (e.g., the role of a student). Norms pertain to *group* expectations (e.g., students in a particular class), whereas culture focuses on the *organization* as a whole (e.g., the student body of a particular college or university). By applying this knowledge to the following two scenarios, you will gain a better appreciation of the distinctiveness, interdependence and richness of these concepts.

Scenario #1: The Social System of your College/University

A) ROLES: the role of a student

    1) What does your college/university expect of students in terms of:

        a) a minimum acceptable G.P.A.?

        b) the proper way to address faculty?

        c) the amount of time it should take to graduate?

        d) scheduling courses for the upcoming semester?

    2) Using Figure 8-5 from the text, describe a role episode that helped you learn an aspect of your role as a student.

B) NORMS: as it relates to this class

    1) What are the norms of this class in relation to:

        a) getting to class on time?

        b) participating in class?

        c) talking with the instructor before or after class?

d) what is acceptable to wear to class?

e) other expected behaviors?

2) Go through your responses to the previous question by predicting what would happen if a classmate violated these norms.

    a) How do you think the instructor would react?

    b) How do you think the rest of the class would react?

    c) Do you think these reactions would prevent others from violating these norms? Explain.

3) The text points out that norms can vary considerably across groups within the same organization. Can you think of other classes you've had at this institution in which the norms were quite different? Explain.

C) CULTURE: of your college/university

1) What values/beliefs does your college/university try to instill in its students?

2) What ceremonies, rituals, or symbols are present at your school to communicate "the way we do things around here"?

3) Culture is considered both a cause and consequence of an organization's success or failure. When you think about a strength or weakness of your college/university, can you attribute part of the credit/blame to its culture?

Scenario #2: The Social System of your organization

For this scenario think of a company you work for or have worked for or an organization that you belong to (not counting your college/university) when answering these questions.

A) ROLES: as an employee

1) What role expectations does your organization have of you in terms of:

    a) acceptable job performance?

b) proper attire to wear to work?

c) arrival and departure time each day?

d) communicating with superiors?

2) Using Figure 8-7 from the text, describe a role episode that helped you learn an aspect of your primary role as an employee.

3) Briefly describe all of the roles you assume in your job (e.g., worker, team leader, liaison to other department).

B) NORMS: as it relates to your department/co-workers/shift

1) What are the norms in your department/co-workers/shift in relation to:

a) taking a sick day?

b) socializing with the boss?

c) taking lunch, coffee, or bathroom breaks?

d) speed at which employees work?

e) any other norms?

2) Go through your responses to the previous question by predicting what would happen if an employee violated these norms.

a) How do you think the employee's boss would react?

b) How do you think the rest of the group would react?

c) Do you think these reactions would prevent others from violating these norms? Explain.

3) Lastly, go through these norms one more time and determine if they coincide or contradict the organization's goals. For those norms that go against the objectives of the organizations, can you think of any ways to change these norms to comply with organizational goals?

C) CULTURE: of your organization

1) As the text points out "an organization's culture can often be traced to its founders." What values/beliefs did your organization's founder(s) try to instill? Are these still the values, beliefs, and attitudes today?

2) What slogans, ceremonies, rituals, legends, stories, or symbols are present at your organization to communicate "the way we do things around here"?

3) How has the external environment (e.g., technological advances, the economy,
   competition, legal developments) affected your organization's culture?

4) How has senior management tried to shape your organization's culture (e.g., hiring/firing, training, policies/procedures, communications) to adapt to its environment?

Exercise 8-3: "Six Sigma and You"

As you know from this chapter, six sigma is an approach to improve organizational processes. Outlined in this chapter are five steps to provide you with an overview of the six sigma system. For this exercise your instructor will break the class into small groups. Each group will apply the five steps outlined in the chapter to your college/university. The questions below will help guide you through this process.

Step 1: Define

In this step your group will identify your college's customers. When you agree on one of the college's customers, identify TWO processes that affect their satisfaction with your college. Processes are aspects of the service provided by your college to its customers. An example of a process for hotel customers would be speed of checkout.

Step 2: Measure

For each process your group identified, how would you measure each one. In other words, how would you obtain numbers that reflect that process? It could be in terms of time (minutes), productivity (units produced), money, ratings, etc…

Step 3: Analyze

Let's assume you collected data for each process you identified above. Based upon the mean and standard deviation for each process, you realize that your college should score better in each area. In this step your group needs to identify THREE reasons why each process may be causing customer dissatisfaction. Basically, what is a limitation of each process?

Step 4: Improve

In this step you group needs to come up with some ideas to improve each process. When you consider what is hurting each of the two processes identified above, what can be done to improve customer satisfaction with these services?

Step 5: Control

In the final step of six sigma you come up with an implementation plan of the solutions your group believes would be the most successful. So in this step, your group needs to outline an implementation of a solution for each process.

Conclusion - reflection

How important do you think it is to identify critical processes related to customer satisfaction?

How important do you think it is to identify quantitative measures of critical processes related to customer satisfaction?

Overall, what is your opinion of the six sigma approach?

Sample multiple-choice items:

1) The functional principle is best reflected in which of the following statements?

   a) The number of hierarchical levels in a company.
   b) Dividing a company into certain groups (e.g., sales, operations, HR).
   c) The number of subordinates per superior.
   d) All of the above apply to the functional principle.

2) If a supervisor has 30 subordinates that report to her, it can be said that she has a(n):

   a) large span of control
   b) high level of functional specialization
   c) high level of centralization
   d) above average level of empowerment

3) Which theory views organizations comparable to a living thing in which it examines the inter-relatedness of the parts of an organization as well as how the organization interacts with its environment?

   a) classical theory
   b) neoclassical theory
   c) systems theory
   d) all three theories have these components

4) Which of the following best represents the coordinating mechanism "standardization of work processes"?

   a) having a supervisor closely monitor employee behavior
   b) extensively training employees in organizational operations
   c) simplifying a task so that it can only be performed in a predetermined manner
   d) allowing employees to talk to each other as long as it's job related

5) Which of the following jobs falls into the technostructure of an organization?

   a) secretary   b) sales clerk
   c) executive vice-president   d) trainer

6) Which of the following is true regarding roles in organizations?

   a) roles are learned quickly
   b) roles are well-defined
   c) roles and jobs are often interchangeable
   d) the person determines the role

7) The ASA cycle refers to:

   a) the social processes in companies to enforce norms
   b) sustaining a culture in companies through recruiting, hiring and turnover
   c) the process by which roles are communicated, adapted and reinforced
   d) the life cycle of growth, maturity and decline of organizations

8) According to Hofstede, which of the following is true regarding U.S. culture:

   a) high in femininity
   b) high in power distance
   c) high in uncertainty avoidance
   d) high in individualism

9) Employees resistance to change will be greater when the change is:

   a) self-initiated rather than imposed by others
   b) revolutionary rather than evolutionary change
   c) additive rather than subtractive change
   d) both "b" and "c"

10) If a company downsizes too many jobs, this condition can be referred to as:

   a) corporate anorexia
   b) an espoused crisis
   c) thin lining
   d) critical shortage phasing

Sample true-false items:

1) The number of hierarchical levels in an organization is called the scalar principle.   T-or-F

2) In examining a company it is important to consider the formal organization from a system's theory approach. T-or-F

3) A role episode is an event in which a person learns about one of his/her roles. T-or-F

4) In non-Western cultures a greater emphasis is placed on the factual accuracy of communication rather than the style of the communication compared to Western cultures. T-or-F

5) In most downsizings the greatest loss of jobs occurs at the strategic apex. T-or-F

Sample short-answer questions:

1) How are classical theory, neoclassical theory, and system theory different? What is the main contribution of each toward our understanding of organizations?

2) Briefly describe the five parts of an organization according to Mintzberg. Provide a job title that falls into each part.

3) What are the four keys to making an effective organizational culture change?

Answer key to the multiple-choice items	**Answer key to true-false items**
1) b	1) T
2) a	2) T
3) c	3) T
4) c	4) F
5) d	5) F
6) a	
7) b	
8) d	
9) b	
10) a	

Chapter 9: Outline

Groups v. teams

Origins of work teams

Amount of information and knowledge available

More educated and trained workforce

Rate of change in work activities

Team halo effect

Level of analysis

Individual (micro)

Team (meso)

Organizational (macro)

Types of teams

Problem-resolution teams

Creative teams

Tactical teams

Ad hoc teams

Multi-team systems

Principles of teamwork

Members provide feedback to and accept it from one another

The willingness, preparedness, and proclivity to back fellow members up during operations

Members' collectively viewing themselves as a group whose success depends on their interaction

Fostering within-team interdependence

Team leadership makes a difference with respect to the performance of the team

Team structure

Diversity in teams

Information diversity

Value diversity

Roles in teams

Leader

Shaper

Worker

Creator

Resource investigator

Monitor-evaluator

Team facilitator

Completer-finisher

130

Four basic functions within a team

Leadership

Work producers

Internal team maintenance

Liaison to people/resources outside the team

Team processes

Socialization

Three psychological concepts of the socialization process

Evaluation

Commitment

Role transition

Five phases of team membership

Investigation

Socialization

Maintenance

Resocialization

Remembrance

Interpersonal processes in teams

Communication

Conflict

Beneficial v. competitive conflict

131

Cohesion

Trust

Shared mental models

Four categories of what is shared

Task-specific knowledge

Task-related knowledge

Knowledge of teammates

Attitudes and beliefs

Groupthink

Team mentality

Decision-making in teams

Multilevel theory of team decision-making

Team informity

Staff validity

Dyadic sensitivity

Virtual teams

Virtual environment

Three characteristics of virtual teams

Electronic communication

Geographical dispersion

Synchronous & asynchronous interaction

Virtual worker & virtual manager

Personnel selection for teams

Taskwork skills v. teamwork skills

Five social skills critical for team members

Gain the group acceptance

Increase group solidarity

Be aware of the group consciousness

Share the group identification

Manage other's impressions of him/her

Big 5 personality traits and team effectiveness

Team training

Thinking

Doing

Feeling

Performance Appraisal in Teams

Social loafing

Free-riding

Sucker effect

Felt dispensability

Peer appraisals

Concept Charts for Chapter 9

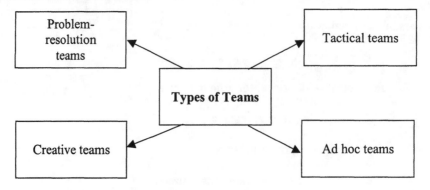

Levels of Analysis

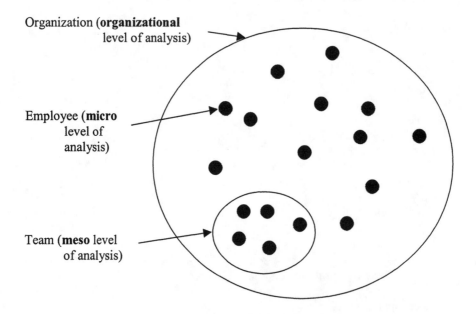

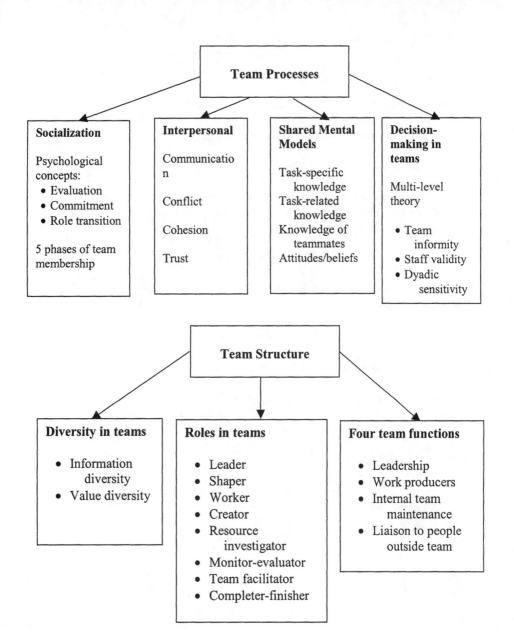

Team Processes

Socialization

Psychological concepts:
- Evaluation
- Commitment
- Role transition

5 phases of team membership

Interpersonal

Communication

Conflict

Cohesion

Trust

Shared Mental Models

Task-specific knowledge
Task-related knowledge
Knowledge of teammates
Attitudes/beliefs

Decision-making in teams

Multi-level theory

- Team informity
- Staff validity
- Dyadic sensitivity

Team Structure

Diversity in teams

- Information diversity
- Value diversity

Roles in teams

- Leader
- Shaper
- Worker
- Creator
- Resource investigator
- Monitor-evaluator
- Team facilitator
- Completer-finisher

Four team functions

- Leadership
- Work producers
- Internal team maintenance
- Liaison to people outside team

1) http://www.nsba.org/sbot/toolkit/LeadTeams.html

This is an article on types of teams.

2) http://www.workteams.unt.edu

This web site is the homepage for the Center for Collaborative Organizations, which was formerly known as the Center for the Study of Work Teams.

3) http://www.hq.nasa.gov/office/hqlibrary/ppm/ppm5.htm

This web site is affiliated with NASA. It provides a listing of various resources on teams.

4) http://www.ucc.uconn.edu/~WWWIOPSY/teams.htm

This web site is an article on teams, specifically focusing on team selection.

5) http://www.seanet.com/~daveg/articles.htm

This web site provides valuable information on virtual teams.

6) http://www.glennparker.com/

This web site is run by a team-building consultant. At this site you will find various teambuilding resources and exercises.

Exercise 9-1: A Capital Offense

This exercise requires you to recall as many state capitals as you can remember. To do this exercise you will need to complete the table on the next page. You will have a set amount of time to complete it by yourself. Then you will do this task again as part of a team. Your instructor will place you into a team. After the exercise is over be prepared to answer the following questions:

1) How many state capitals did you identify by yourself? _____

2) How many state capitals did your team identify? _____

3) Based on this exercise, what are the advantages of completing a task as part of a team as compared to by yourself?

4) This chapter talks about the roles often found in teams. Describe each team member in the context of the eight roles identified in the chapter (leader, shaper, worker, creator, resource investigator, monitor-evaluator, team facilitator, completer-finisher).

5) There are four major interpersonal processes in team: communication, conflict, cohesion, and trust. Evaluate your team in the context of these processes.

6) Where there any barriers to team performance (e.g., socializing)? What would you recommend to overcome these barriers?

STATE CAPITALS ?

Alabama	Alaska	Arizona	Arkansas	California
Colorado	Connecticut	Delaware	Florida	Georgia
Hawaii	Idaho	Illinois	Indiana	Iowa
Kansas	Kentucky	Louisiana	Maine	Maryland
Massachusetts	Michigan	Minnesota	Mississippi	Missouri
Montana	Nebraska	Nevada	New Hampshire	New Jersey
New Mexico	New York	North Carolina	North Dakota	Ohio
Oklahoma	Oregon	Pennsylvania	Rhode Island	South Carolina
South Dakota	Tennessee	Texas	Utah	Vermont
Virginia	Washington	West Virginia	Wisconsin	Wyoming

Record how many state capitals you identified by yourself: _____

Record how many state capitals your team identified : _____

Exercise 9-2: Be a Sport

When people hear the word "team" the first thing that pops into many of their minds is a sport team. Many of us have played on various sport teams and continue to do so as well as watch them in person or on television. This chapter focuses on teams at work. This exercise is geared towards seeing if the ideas presented in this chapter apply to athletic teams as well.

To complete this exercise your instructor will divide the class into small groups. Each group will be assigned to a team at your college/university. Depending upon the size of your group, one (or two) of you will interview the coach, another student or two will interview the captain of this team, and the others will interview other players on the team.

When preparing for the interview your team should look at the chapter outline. Identify a handful of key chapter topics that you want to collect information on. For example a chapter relevant question to ask a coach would be, "besides talent, what other factors do you look at when assessing potential players?" (personnel selection) A possible question for the team captain would be, "when you think a teammate is not giving his or her all (social loafing), how do you handle it?" A possible question for a player on the team would be, "how does the coach evaluate individual performance in a team sport?" (performance appraisal in teams).

Once the interviews are completed, your group can integrate your findings in a report or presentation to the class, depending upon your instructor's preference.

Exercise 9-3: Teams in Action

This exercise will give you an opportunity to work as part of a team as well as observe and evaluate another team's performance.

To complete this assignment, your instructor will divide the class into an even number of groups. Each group should range in size from 4 to 6 students. Half of the groups will be considered problem-resolution teams, whereas the other groups will be observing a problem-resolution team for scenario #1. For scenario #2, the groups will switch roles.

As observers you will watch the team interact. Then you will evaluate the team using the evaluation form on the next page. Please note that the evaluation criteria are directly related to the 5 principles of effective teamwork discussed in the text.

139

Scenario #1: Problem-Resolution: Your group has been given an opportunity to meet with the president of your college/university. The president would like your group to present to him/her the most pressing problem, from the students' view, that this college/university needs to be corrected. Your team has to decide what one aspect of the college/university you would like to change. Further, not only does your group have to agree on the problem to be changed, the team has to justify why it should be changed, how to change it, as well as the advantages and disadvantages in making this change.

Scenario #2: Creative Teams: You and your group are one of several research & development teams for Widget World Incorporated (WWI). Your task is to come up with a new product idea that will make the company millions of dollars. As you know WWI already makes a wide variety of unique products: the thermometer-turkey baster, the combo mechanical pencil & dinner fork (so you can eat while you work), glow in the dark golf balls, and the ever popular paper clip - nose hair clippers. Your team has to think of a *new unusual product* that would most likely be sold for less than $15, could be mass produced, and would sell to a large audience.

Teamwork Evaluation Form

Please rate the team you are observing using the following scale:

1	2	3	4	5
poor		satisfactory		excellent

#1: *Teamwork implies that members provide feedback to and accept it from one another.*

___ 1. Participation from all team members was encouraged.
___ 2. Constructive criticism was valued rather than dismissed.

#2: *Teamwork implies the willingness, preparedness, and proclivity to back fellow members up during operations.*

___ 3. The team members took the initiative to help each other.
___ 4. Team members showed support for each other's ideas.

#3: *Teamwork involves group members' collectively viewing themselves as a group whose success depends on their interaction.*

140

___ 5. Team members seemed more concerned about the team's success rather than individual recognition.

___ 6. The team recognized that one member could not and should not "carry" the team in order to be highly effective.

#4: Teamwork means fostering within-team interdependence.

___ 7. Cooperation within the team was stressed.

___ 8. Every team member was viewed and treated as equally important to the team's success.

#5: Team leadership makes a difference with respect to the performance of the team.

___ 9. The team leader came across as a facilitator rather than a dictator.

___ 10. The team leader was able to provide and accept feedback.

___ **TOTAL SCORE**

Sample multiple-choice items:

1) One of the 3 main reasons that the use of work teams has increased is because:

   a) employees today like working in groups rather than alone
   b) companies can now save money by using teams
   c) discrimination charges are less likely to occur today in team-based companies
   d) employees are more educated today and thus more capable of meeting team roles

2) Meso, micro and macro are all types of:

   a) ad hoc team structures
   b) levels of analysis
   c) stages of team development
   d) phases of team decision-making

3) A ___ team is one that is designed to carry out a task (e.g., Los Angeles Lakers).

   a) tactical
   b) problem-solving
   c) creative
   d) virtual

4) ___ diversity refers to the extent to which team members have diverse experiences and areas of expertise.

   a) Value
   b) Cultural
   c) Information
   d) Staff

5) All of the following are roles found in teams EXCEPT:

   a) shaper
   b) creator
   c) worker
   d) informer

6) When an individual in a team moves from one phase of team membership to the next, this is referred to as:

    a) Role transition
    b) Evaluation
    c) Commitment
    d) Validity

7) The two basic types of conflict found in teams are:

    a) competitive; cooperative
    b) beneficial; competitive
    c) beneficial; confrontational
    d) competitive; confrontational

8) The general level of how much a given team knows about the task at hand is called:

    a) staff validity
    b) dyadic sensitivity
    c) team informity
    d) task-related knowledge

9) In selecting team members all of the following should be considered EXCEPT:

    a) general mental ability
    b) social skills
    c) the big 5 personality variables
    d) all of the above should be considered

10) In studying team performance, some members may reduce their efforts so they don't contribute much more than anyone else contributes. This is known as the:

    a) free rider effect
    b) sucker effect
    c) felt dispensability effect
    d) social loafer effect

Sample true-false questions:

1) An ad hoc team refers to teams that are used to market or advertise company products and/or services. T-or-F

2) The most critical aspects of team diversity are in regards to diversity based upon age, sex and race. T-or-F

3) The liaison role is one of the basic functions within a team. T-or-F

4) Groupthink is considered a positive byproduct of shared mental models in teams. T-or-F

5) E-mail would be an example of synchronous communication. T-or-F

Sample short-answer questions:

1) What does level of analysis refer to? What are the types of levels?

2) Summarize the basic principles of teamwork.

3) What are the unique features of a good team training program?

Answer key to the multiple-choice items	Answer key to true-false items
1) d	1) F
2) b	2) F
3) a	3) T
4) c	4) F
5) d	5) F
6) a	
7) b	
8) c	
9) d	
10) b	

Chapter 10: Outline

Job satisfaction

Global job satisfaction

Job facet satisfaction

Job Descriptive Index

Minnesota Satisfaction Questionnaire

Brief's model of job satisfaction

Positive affect

Objective job circumstances

Five categories of emotions

Emotional contagion

Relationship of satisfaction with performance, turnover & absence

Withdrawal behavior

Job involvement

Organizational commitment

Affective component

Continuance component

Normative component

145

Occupational commitment

Organizational commitment

Work commitment

Organizational justice

Distributive justice

Equity rule

Equality rule

Need rule

Individualism v. Collectivism

Procedural justice

Individual's "voice" in the process

Structural components of the process

Interactional justice

Interpersonal justice

Informational justice

Organizational citizenship behavior (prosocial, extra-role, contextual)

Five main dimensions

Altruism

Conscientiousness

Courtesy

Sportsmanship

Civic virtue

Dispositional origins

Conscientiousness

Agreeableness

Situational antecedents

Organizational justice

The psychological contract

Two principles of the psychological contract

Mutuality

Reciprocity

Transactional contracts

Relational contracts

Symmetrical v. Asymmetrical power

Consequences of violating the psychological contract

Move from relational to transactional

Voice

Silence

Retreat

Destruction

Exit

Individual responses to downsizing

Terminated personnel

Surviving personnel

Use of contingent workers

The psychology of mergers and acquisitions

Merger

Acquisition

Parent

Target

Three phases in the merger process

Precombination

Combination

Postcombination

Antisocial behavior in the workplace (organizational deviance, workplace incivility)

Thermodynamics of revenge

Violation of the psychological contract

Perceived organizational injustice

Venting

Dissipation

Fatigue

Explosion

148

Violence in the workplace

Occupational homicide

Aggression

Profile approach to identifying workplace aggressors

Situational factors related to workplace violence

Strategies dealing with violence in the workplace

Preventative strategies

Reactive strategies

Rehabilitative strategies

Job Satisfaction

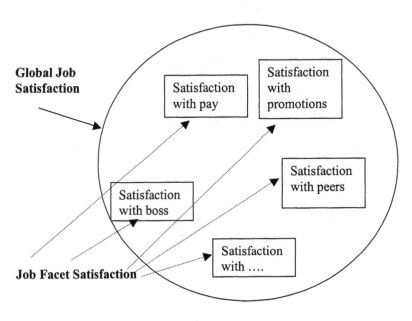

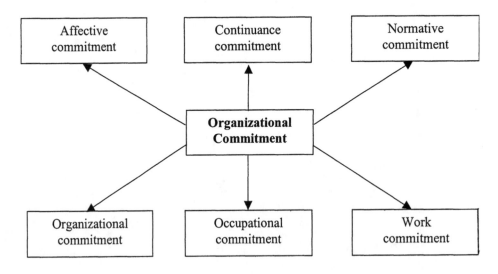

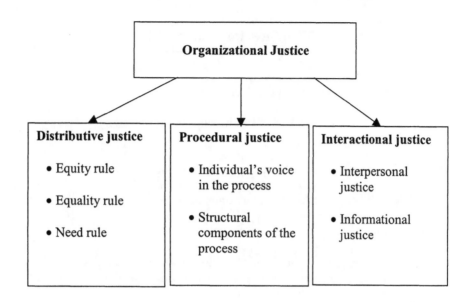

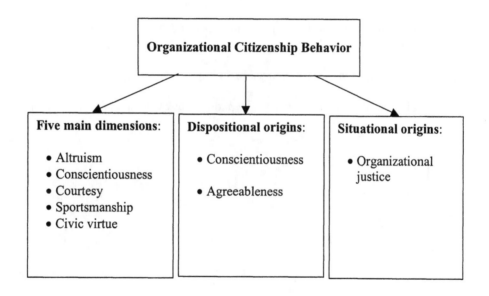

Web Sites for Chapter 10

1) http://www.manpower.com/mpcom/index.jsp

This is the web site for Manpower, which is the most well known temporary staffing service organization.

2) http://www.osha-slc.gov/SLTC/workplaceviolence/index.html

This is OSHA's web site for information on workplace violence.

3) http://www.bgsu.edu/departments/psych/JDI/

This web site provides information on the Job Descriptive Index, including the history of this instrument, a reference list of research articles on the JDI as well as purchasing this measure of job satisfaction.

4) http://www.mareport.com/mar/news_updates.cfm

This web site is dedicated to providing news updates on mergers and acquisitions.

5) http://stats.bls.gov/news.release/conemp.nr0.htm

This web site is a report from the Department of Labor on the prevalence of contingent workers.

Exercise 10-1: The Scales of Justice

This chapter begins with a discussion of organizational justice. More specifically, the chapter describes the various types of organizational justice: procedural, distributive, and interactional. The following case requires you to differentiate among these types of organizational justices by applying them to a case study. Please read the following case study, then answer the questions following.

Black Mack Trucking Company is an interstate trucking company that transports a variety of goods and services. The company employs over 500 truckers. The company is experiencing a common HR problem. The turnover rate for truckers has gone up dramatically over the past 12 months. This increase in turnover corresponds to the time when the company implemented a new compensation system. Under the new system, starting salary is negotiated during the selection process. Previously, there was a set starting wage, which wasn't open to debate. The company is hoping to get new hires to agree on the lowest wage possible. Results, however, have varied based upon the negotiating skills of the new hire as well as the person's sex and racial background. The company is much more generous in bargaining when the new hire is female or a minority. The company is trying to avoid any clashes with the EEOC. Not surprising, the average starting salary for female truck drivers is $550 per week, for minorities it's $500 per week, and for white males it's $425 per week. Even though this practice violates the Equal Pay Act of 1963 ("equal pay for equal work"), the company is more concerned with increasing minority representation in their workforce. The company does not feel comfortable explaining their approach to determining starting salary. Thus, when an employee tries to challenge the system, the HR director simply states, "The company views salary as a private matter. We don't feel it is appropriate to justify perceived differences in starting salary. You agreed to your amount during the interviews. If you are no longer happy with your wage, it's unfortunate, but there's nothing we can do. If you don't like it, no one is stopping you from leaving." It didn't take long for employees to notice the differences in starting salary as well as the poor explanation by the HR director. Many employees quit right after the above-mentioned spiel.

153

The new compensation system also covers bonus pay. The following memo was distributed to all truckers describing this new pay system.

Memorandum

To: All truckers

From: Marty Martin - Human Resources Director

Subject: New Bonus System

Date: January 1, 2004

The company has decided to implement a new bonus system, effective immediately. The new system is designed to reward you for making deliveries on time (within 1 hour of the scheduled arrival time). The company firmly believes that on-time deliveries are the key to repeat business, which in turn leads to a successful and prosperous organization. The more successful our company, the more we can reward you, our valued employees.

The system is quite simple. At the end of each month the percentage of times your deliveries were on time will be calculated. Based upon your percentage, you will receive a bonus check according to the following table:

Percentage On-Time	Bonus for the Month
100%	$250
95 to 99%	$200
85 to 94%	$125
75 to 84%	$50
under 75%	$0

For example, if you make 20 deliveries this month and 18 of them are made on-time your percentage for the month would be 90% (18 divided by 20). You would receive a $125 bonus check.

If you have any questions or concerns, please feel free to give me a call at extension 310. I think this system will work to everyone's advantage!

At first glance, the bonus system seemed fair, however, the day-to-day operation of the system had several problems:

1) *Determining an estimated arrival time is very subjective.* For example, a delivery to Manhattan, NY takes much longer than a delivery to Manhattan, KS even if the mileage is equivalent. Also, a delivery at night is also less time consuming than at rush hour.

2) *Keeping accurate records of on-time deliveries is not simple.* Dispatchers now have to call every delivery site to check when the delivery arrived as well as maintain accurate records. The dispatchers felt they were overworked all ready. Numerous errors have been detected.

3) *The quality of the trucks vary considerably.* Some truckers have a lower percentage of on-time deliveries because their truck breaks down. They feel they shouldn't be penalized for a flat tire or an overheated radiator.

4) *Safety is being compromised.* Many truckers are driving much more aggressively (e.g., speeding) to make sure they get there on time. The number of accidents has doubled since the new bonus system has been implemented.

Since the new bonus system has been implemented, on-time deliveries has increased by 30%, however costs due to accidents and turnover have exceeded any gains.

QUESTIONS

(A) Starting Salary:

1) How fair is the starting salary system in terms of procedural justice?

2) How fair is the starting salary system in terms of distributive justice?

3) How fair is the starting salary system in terms of interactional justice?

4) How can the company improve how they determine starting salaries?

155

(B) Bonus Pay:

    1) Does the **bonus pay system** seem to have procedural, interactional and/or distributive justice?

    2) Can the bonus pay system be improved and still motivate truckers to make deliveries on time?

Exercise 10-2: The Good Soldier

Another major topic in this chapter is **organizational citizenship behavior** (OCB). OCB refers to going beyond job requirements and giving extra to the organization. The text mentions the five dimensions most often associated with OCB: altruism, conscientiousness, courtesy, sportsmanship, and civic virtue. This exercise will help you distinguish among these dimensions as well as illustrating the breadth of OCB. On a blank sheet of paper:

PART 1: Write your current or most recent job title

    Then list the top 5 task requirements of this job: (keep in mind, this refers to things you were **required** to do; they should be listed in the job description)

PART 2: OCB activities

    Next, think of 5 behaviors that you do or did in this job that were not task requirements, but for the benefit of the organization (e.g., voluntarily joining committees). Then classify each behavior as either: altruism, conscientiousness, courtesy, sportsmanship, or civic virtue.

PART 3: Negative job behaviors

The text discusses OCB actions that are positive influences on the organization. However, employees can also engage in other behaviors, not listed in their job description, which are detrimental to the organization (e.g., saying disparaging comments about others). Basically, anti-OCB actions. In this section, think of at least three examples of negative job behaviors that you have observed in your current or former job.

156

At this point it is pretty clear that employees can engage in numerous job behaviors, some of which have positive effects on the organization and some of which have damaging effects on the organization.

Questions:

1) When you think about how your job performance was evaluated, were these positive and negative job behaviors mentioned above included in your evaluation? If no, why do you think they were not?

2) How would you revise your performance evaluation to include these factors?

3) How much weight should be given to these factors in determining pay raises and promotions?

4) Can we really measure these positive and negative extra-role behaviors accurately? If no, are the above issues no longer valid?

Exercise 10-3: Power, Rage, & Anger

The last section of the chapter discusses violence in the workplace. The text indicates that the frequency and severity of workplace violence is escalating across the nation. Thus, the importance of being prepared to handle workplace violence as well as implementing strategies to reduce workplace violence is critical. Listed below are two scenarios that deal with workplace violence. Please read each of the scenarios and then address the questions that follow. These scenarios should help you grasp the complexities of this volatile issue.

Scenario #1: "Frustrated, Fired Frank"

Frank Lee worked for Kirby Tires Inc. for the past 18 years. He started out on the assembly line making tires and was promoted to foreman around 6 years ago. Frank has a wife and three kids, two of whom are in college. Frank's job performance was excellent up until last year. Last Christmas his problems began. His parents left his house after Christmas dinner. On their way home, their car was blindsided by a drunk driver. His mother died instantly, while his father hung on for several weeks in intensive care before passing away.

Frank hasn't been the same since. The production rate of his line dropped off by 19%. He called in sick 13 times over the past 6 months. He was late at least 30 minutes every day for the past two weeks. Further, his attitude was very low; he never smiled, and seemed to be totally depressed. The company completely ignored the performance problems, because of his long productive history with the company. Nothing was even mentioned to him before last week. Late last week he received the following notice:

Dear Mr. F. Lee,

It has come to my attention that you have been repeatedly late in getting to work over the past few days. If this behavior continues, you will be immediately terminated.

Sincerely,
Kyle Rogers, HR Director

Frank came in late on Monday and Tuesday. Tuesday afternoon he received the following:

Dear Mr. F. Lee,

It has come to my attention that you have been repeatedly late this week as well. Your employment at Kirby Tires is terminated, effective immediately. All benefits you receive will be stopped by week's end.

Sincerely,
Kyle Rogers, HR Director

Frank did not handle the firing very well. On Wednesday morning Frank showed up for work, on time by the way, with a shotgun. He killed Kyle Rogers and then turned the gun on himself. The company is in shock.

Questions:

1) If you were the HR director, would you have handled the Frank Lee situation differently? If so, how?

2) What should the company do to reduce the likelihood of this ever happening again?

3) What steps would you take to help the company recover from such a tragic incident?

Scenario #2: "The customer is always right"

Violence in the workplace became a reality for Kloggy Klothes Stores. Marisa Cupman, a customer, came into the store wanting to return a blouse she bought. The sales clerk, Jamie Johnson, asked Marisa for her sales receipt. Marisa replied, "I don't have a receipt. This was given to me as a birthday gift a few days ago." Jamie thought a moment of the company's return policy:

1. No returns without a receipt.
2. No returns if the merchandise was purchased more than 3 months ago.
3. No returns if the merchandise looks worn.

Jamie then took the garment from Marisa's hand to examine it. Jamie recognized that the blouse was part of the company's own line of clothes, which just came out last week. The blouse looked like it had never been washed. Further, since the blouse is so new, its price had not changed.

Jamie handed the blouse back to Marisa and said, "I'm sorry there's nothing I can do. No returns without a receipt." Marisa became visibly upset and asked to speak to the manager. Jamie, not wanting to bother the manager, stated, "There's no one you can talk to. The manager is gone for the week. You'll have to come back then." Marisa replied with numerous profanities. Jamie, upset by this reaction, reached into her pocket and threw Marisa a quarter and said, "Call someone who cares." Marisa threw the blouse in Jamie's face and increased her use of profanity. Jamie responded with similar comments and before long the two were fighting in the middle of the aisle. Other customers in the store were outraged. The manager tried to intervene, but it was too late. The damage was done. Marisa has filed a lawsuit against the store for pain and suffering.

Questions:

1) How should Jamie have handled the situation to avoid such a conflict? Keep in mind she did enforce the company's return policy.

2) Are there any implications for human resources in terms of orientation, training, termination, selection or other I/O psychology areas to reduce the probability of this ever happening again?

3) If you were the store manager, what would you do for damage control? Many customers were visibly upset and about to leave the store upon seeing the incidence.

Sample multiple-choice items:

1) One day Julie comes by your office and says "I really enjoy the people I work with but overall I really can't stand this job." This statement suggests that Julie has:

   a) high global job satisfaction and low job involvement
   b) low global job satisfaction and high job facet satisfaction
   c) low global job satisfaction and high OCB
   d) low job involvement and high job facet satisfaction

2) Jim will never quit his job because he feels a sense of obligation to be loyal to his company, whereas Dana will never leave her job because she will never find another job that pays her so well. This scenario indicates that Jim has high ___ organizational commitment, whereas Dana has high ___ organizational commitment.

   a) normative; continuance
   b) continuance; affective
   c) affective; normative
   d) continuous; normative

3) George is an architect. For George his life is architecture. He reads about it, talks about it, and thinks about it all of the time. Not surprisingly George's job means everything to him. Basically George has high:

   a) job facet satisfaction
   b) continuance commitment
   c) job involvement
   d) OCB

4) Christine is the top performer in her department. Because of her excellence, she was awarded a $2000 pay raise. Don is a marginal performer in the same department, He was awarded a $1700 pay raise. Christine is upset with the small difference between her raise and Don's raise. She feels this decision has low:

a) interactional justice
b) procedural justice
c) interpersonal justice
d) distributive justice

5) Informational justice is a type of:

a) procedural justice
b) distributive justice
c) interpersonal justice
d) interactional justice

6) Dominic is a great employee. He never gossips, never complains and keeps things in a proper perspective. Which OCB component is Dominic high in?

a) sportsmanship
b) civic virtue
c) conscientiousness
d) altruism

7) A long-term employee with a high level of affective organizational commitment most likely has which type of a psychological contract with his/her employer?

a) transactional
b) relational
c) continual
d) interactional

8) Employees that remain after a downsizing are likely to have:

a) higher levels of organizational commitment since the company kept them
b) higher levels of performance since they are more motivated
c) higher levels of stress because they have more work to do
d) all of the above

9) If Wal-Mart decided to acquire Reebok, then Reebok would be the:

   a) parent
   b) child
   c) target
   d) option

10) Situational factors related to workplace violence include all of the following EXCEPT:

   a) high job involvement
   b) high workplace temperatures
   c) high noise
   d) high alcohol use

Sample true-false items:

1) The Job Descriptive Index is a measure of job involvement. T-or-F

2) Hiring the best applicant for a job would be consistent with the equity rule of distributive justice. T-or-F

3) Mutuality refers to the extent to which workers and employers share beliefs regarding specific aspects of the psychological contract. T-or-F

4) Combination is the first phase of the merger process. T-or-F

5) Most employees that fit the profile of perpetrators of workplace violence do not actually commit workplace violence. T-or-F

Sample short-answer questions:

1) What is Brief's model of job satisfaction?

2) Differentiate among occupational, organizational and job commitment.

3) What are the contributing factors to the "thermodynamics of revenge?" Describe the process.

Answer key to the multiple–choice items	Answer key to true-false items
1) b	1) F
2) a	2) T
3) c	3) T
4) d	4) F
5) d	5) T
6) a	
7) b	
8) c	
9) c	
10) a	

Chapter 11: Outline

Occupational health

"Mental health of the industrial worker" (by Kornhauser)

Organizational health

Intrinsic value of work

Instrumental value of work

Positive psychology

Environmental influences on mental health

Opportunity for control

Two key elements

Opportunity for skill use

Externally generated goals

Environmental variety

Environmental clarity

Two aspects of clarity

Availability of money

Physical security

Opportunity for interpersonal contact

Perceptions & cognitions: The appraisal process

 Primary appraisal

 Secondary appraisal

Response to stress

 Physiological

 Psychological

  Organizational sleepwalkers

 Behavioral

  Five broad categories

Consequences of stress

Properties of the person as stress mediators

 Type A v. Type B personality

 Internal v. External locus of control

Properties of the situation as stress mediators

 Social support

 Additional situational buffers

Prevention & intervention of stress

 Stress management

 Prevention programs

 Stress intervention initiatives

Work/family conflict

Cross-cultural differences

The effect of work on family

The effect of family on work

The family-work interaction

Conceptual models of the relationship between work & family

Spillover Model

Compensation Model

Segmentation Model

Gender differences in work/family conflict

Assistance in reducing work/family conflict

Adjusting work schedules

Child-care centers

The Family and Medical Leave Act

Elder-care programs

Dual-career families

Gender differences

Differential investment in career and family

Lack of temporal control

Work schedules

Shift work

Rotating shifts

Biochronology

Forward v. backward rotation

Flextime

Coretime

Flexband

Compressed workweek

Alcoholism and drug abuse in the workplace

Substance abuse

Americans with Disabilities Act (ADA)

Employee assistance programs (EAP)

Psychological effects of unemployment

Intended consequences of employment

Unintended consequences of employment

Unemployment & loss of discretionary control

Relationship between unemployment & mental health

Child labor and exploitation

Use of child labor in foreign countries

Fair Labor Standards Act

Environmental influences on mental health

Opportunity for control	Opportunity for skill use	Externally generated goals
Environmental variety	Environmental clarity	Availability of money
Physical security	Opportunity for interpersonal contact	Valued social position

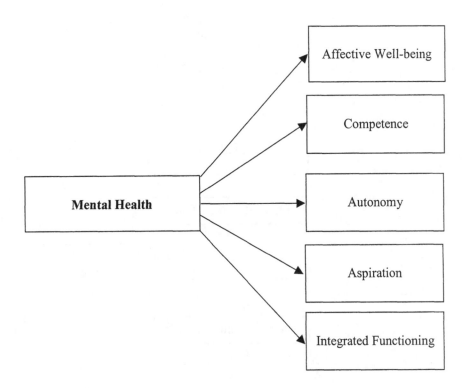

Model of Stress

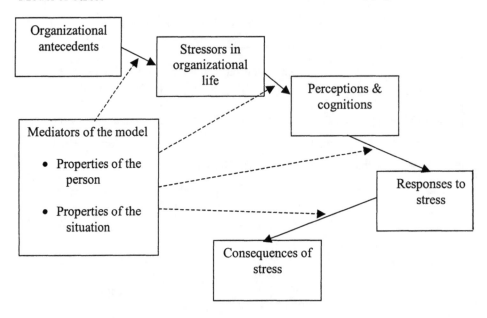

Work/Family Conflict

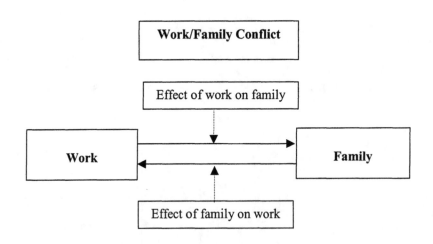

Web Sites for Chapter 11

1) http://stats.bls.gov/bls/employment.htm

A Bureau of Labor Statistics' web site that provides information on unemployment.

2) http://www4.law.cornell.edu/uscode/29/ch28.html

This web site provides the text of the Family and Medical Leave Act.

3) http://www.positivepsychology.org/

This web site will provide you with access to resources on positive psychology, which is mentioned in the beginning of this chapter.

4) http://www.dol.gov/dol/topic/youthlabor/index.htm

This web site is run by the U.S. Department of Labor. At this site you will be able to find considerable information on child labor.

5) http://www.cdc.gov/niosh/stresswk.html

This web site is a report by the National Institute for Occupational Safety and Health (NIOSH) on workplace stress.

Exercise 11-1: "To Be or Not To Be" Employed

One of the most important sections of Chapter 11 deals with the psychological effects of unemployment. The following case study requires you to apply this material as well as discuss the implications of unemployment to an organization. Please read the following case study and answer the questions at the end.

You are the vice-president of human resources for a large manufacturing company. The company produces silverware. The company is able to manufacture approximately 12,000 table settings each month. The production process is relatively simple. Basically, all workers need to do is monitor various aspects of the system. They need to make sure there is enough raw material to produce the silverware. Also, they need to check for defects, work the stamping machine, adjust the rate of production, package the silverware, and load it onto trucks.

The company employs 600 production workers. Less than 5% of these workers have a college education. About 40% of them do not have a high school diploma. You suspect a considerable percentage of your workforce is illiterate. Additionally, most of your workers are male (85%) and over 40 years of age (median age = 43). The company is located in a relatively small northeastern city (population 25,000). The company was founded in this city over 80 years ago. The unemployment rate in the town is 7.9%, which is well above the national average. Your company is one of the few positive economic aspects of the community.

Unfortunately, the profits for the company have been steadily declining. Foreign competition and the increasing price of silver has lowered profits consistently over the past 10 years. Last year the company just broke even. If things do not change soon the company could be near bankruptcy within 5 to 10 years. The company's president has recently returned from a conference on technological advances in mass production. At the conference she learned about a new computer-automated production system. The system will be available in about 6 to 9 months. The cost of the technology is around $3 million, however the new equipment could save the company about $10 million per year in reduced labor costs. If the company purchases the new technology, the company will be able to maintain production standards and quality with a lot less employees.

The president has scheduled a meeting for early next week for all vice-presidents to discuss the purchase of the new technology. If the company decides to acquire the new system, which you feel they most likely will, you will be in the unenviable position of laying off countless production workers. You must be prepared to deal with this decision.

Questions:

1) How should the company decide which employees to lay off?

2) How should they be notified of the layoff?

3) How do you think the soon-to-be laid off employees will react to the news?

4) How do you think the surviving employees will react?

5) Do you think the layoff will affect the community? Should this be a concern if it does?

6) Should the company offer workshops to the employees that will be laid off to help them deal with the job loss and assist them in securing re-employment? What would be the content of the workshop?

Exercise 11-2: The Joy of Stress

Another section of Chapter 11 deals with **work stress***; it's causes, responses, consequences, and other elements related to stress. The following scenario describes two individuals who are experiencing work stress. Read the case and answer the questions that follow.*

You are the HR manager of a retail store that sells clothes for both men and women of all ages. The store has approximately 75 sales clerks. The store is open from 8 am to 9 pm Monday through Saturday. On Sundays, the store is open from 10 am to 6 pm. The store is located in a large metropolitan area.

The first employee that has stopped by your office to complain about feeling stressed out is Jose DeMarco. Jose's job is relatively simple. When clothes arrive at the store, they are sent to Jose in a large bin with wheels. Jose attaches a theft detector device to every article of clothing. The device is the same for all the clothes. The device is applied rather easily. A piece of the clothing is put in a section of a large machine, Jose pushes a button, and the machine basically "staples" the security device. Once Jose finishes all the clothes in the bin, he gets another bin and starts over. Jose doesn't have to worry about problems with co-workers; he works completely alone. He is not supervised. His only requirement is that he must finish at least 1 bin per hour, which is somewhat demanding. As mentioned earlier, Jose works alone in a relatively small room. Unfortunately the room doesn't have any windows or air conditioning. It does get pretty hot in there during the summer months. The air can be quite stale. Further, the room is noisy from the "stapling" machine. Jose claims the job has affected him in numerous ways: high blood pressure, ulcers, frustration and boredom. Jose is seriously thinking about quitting. You've also noticed from his personnel file, Jose has been absent more often this year than last, he's struggled on several occasions to meet his one bin per hour quota, and he has left work early 3 times already this year.

The second employee that stopped by your office to complain about job stress is Kim Chi. Kim is a sales clerk. Kim enjoys interacting with customers, working the register, maintaining a clean and orderly store area, and setting up displays. Kim has been trained to work in two adjacent areas of the store: women's sportswear and girls' formalwear. Kim often works in one section part of a given work day and the other section the other part of the day. There are different supervisors for each section of the store. Further, Kim's work schedule requires her to work three day shifts per week (8 am to 5 pm) and two night shifts (2 pm to 9 pm). Kim has a difficult time getting along with the night supervisor of girls' formalwear. Kim thinks the tension is the result of the supervisor's prejudice towards Asian Americans. Another problem Kim has is that she often feels pulled in different directions. Some days she starts work in women's sportswear and the girls' formalwear supervisor tells her to stop what she's doing and work in formalwear. If she does move over to the formalwear, the sportswear supervisor gets upset. If she refuses, the formalwear supervisor gets upset. She often feels stuck-in-the-middle. Another complaint Kim has is that she feels the store is understaffed on the weekends. She often has a huge line of customers waiting at the register. Lastly, Kim often feels overworked. For example, last Tuesday she started work at 8 am. A note was waiting for her from the supervisor. The note told her to redo all the displays in sportswear, and rack two bins of new clothes that came in yesterday before she leaves at five. Moreover, she was the only one scheduled to work that day in sportswear, which happened to be the last day of a sales promotion. Needless to say, she was swamped, and completely stressed out by the day's end. Not surprising her displays were not as impressive as they have been in the past and her supervisor criticized her for them. Kim indicated that something has to change soon. She can't keep up this pace. She leaves work exhausted, often times with a splitting headache. Her morale is getting lower and lower. The other day she yelled at a co-worker, which she has never done before. This week she has been late twice.

Questions:

1) What are the stressors for:

    a) Jose?

174

b) Kim?

2) The text mentions two types of stressors: task content and role properties. Which type fits with each person?

    a) Jose
    b) Kim

3) The chapter mentions 3 types of responses to stress: physiological, psychological, and behavioral. Identify and then classify each response to stress into one of these three categories for:

    a) Jose
    b) Kim

4) Lastly, what organizational interventions would you recommend to help Jose and/or
Kim to reduce/prevent or help them cope with stress?

    a) Jose
    b) Kim

Exercise 11-3: Love on the Rocks

Another aspect of this chapter deals with the difficulties of work, and family. The purpose of this exercise is to help you explore the difficulties associated with work/family conflicts. Please read the following scenarios and respond to the questions below.

Scenario #1: Marc and Cleo

Marc and Cleo are expecting their first child in about five months. They have decided that one of them should stay home with the baby for at least one year. After the baby is one year old, the child will be put in daycare. The trouble is who should stay home. Both of them are on the fast track to the executive suite. Their salaries are comparable. They know whomever takes a year off will have no guarantee of a job when they want to return to work. One of them will sacrifice their career development. If they split the year (six months each), both of them will sacrifice their careers.

Questions:

1) If you were in Marc or Cleo's position, how would you decide?

2) Do you think parents should sacrifice their careers for child rearing?

Scenario #2: Brad and Hanna

Brad and Hanna are expecting their third child in a few months. For their first two children, Hanna quit work for five years to raise the kids until they were old enough for preschool. This time off hurt Hanna's career advancement as a graphic design specialist. Hanna has been working now for around six years and her career once again is about to take off. She is very excited about her career. This pregnancy, however, was not planned. Due to Hanna's sacrifices, Brad did quite well in his career. Currently, he is a junior partner in a CPA firm and he's the odds on favorite to get the next senior partner position. If he takes off for an extended period (6 months or more) for this child, he believes the senior partners will see the move as a lack of commitment to the firm. All of the senior partners sacrificed family involvement for their careers, why shouldn't Brad? Senior partnership means much more money and prestige. Hanna and Brad agree that one of them should take time off to raise the child for at least a year, but who? Hanna feels she's sacrificed her career already and now it's Brad's turn. She wants a chance to be successful in her career. He has had his chance. Brad disagrees. Hanna's previous sacrifice has gotten him to where he is today. If he makes this sacrifice, he feels Hanna's sacrifice would be wasted. Therefore, Brad thinks Hanna should stay home with the baby.

Questions:

1) Who should take off: Brad or Hanna? Explain.

2) Should organizations ask applicants about their family responsibilities or intentions? Should this information to screen out applicants that may cause problems?

3) What programs or interventions could organizations adopt to reduce/eliminate the conflicts mentioned in the above scenarios?

4) Should organizations really care about family/work conflict? Should this really be a concern to a company? Explain the pros and cons.

5) How do you think organizational accommodations for work/family conflicts affect:

    a) organizational culture

    b) organizational commitment

    c) stress

Self-Test for Chapter 11

Sample multiple-choice items:

1) When you think about work, you think about salary, benefits, and status; then work has a high ___ value to you.

    a) external   b) evaluative
    c) instrumental   d) intrinsic

2) As a component of mental health, aspiration refers to:

    a) being very achievement-oriented
    b) demonstrating adequate resources to handling life's challenges
    c) a situation of high pleasure and high arousal
    d) exhibiting balance, harmony, and inner relatedness

3) "Sick building syndrome" is an example of a(n):

    a) organizational antecedent to stress
    b) task content stressor in organizational life
    c) role property stressor in organizational life
    d) eustress

4) A student receives a "F" on an exam. She attributes the grade to her inability to make the necessary time to study. This scenario represents:

    a) a Type A personality
    b) a Type B personality
    c) an internal locus of control
    d) an external locus of control

5) In terms of the relationship between work and family which model suggests that stress in one context will affect stress in the other context?

a) compensation model
b) spillover model
c) segmentation model
d) congruency model

6) Which law allows employees 12 weeks off (unpaid) for the birth of a child?

a) Pregnancy Protection Act
b) Equal Employment Opportunity Act
c) Family and Medical Leave Act
d) Newborn Child Workplace Act

7) Amy can start her workday anytime she wishes as long as she is in her office by 11 a.m. and works 8 hours before she leaves. This is an example of a:

a) compressed workweek
b) telecommuting agreement
c) shift work schedule
d) flextime arrangement

8) Former drug users have legal protection in terms of employment under the:

a) ADA
b) EAP
c) FLSA
d) Former drug users do not have legal protection in employment

9) All of the following are unintended consequences of employment EXCEPT:

a) Provides a time structure to your day
b) It enforces activity for the individual
c) Provides regular shared experiences with people outside of one's family
d) It allows one to earn a living

10) Which of the following is true regarding child labor?

   a) U.S. companies are not allowed to use child labor in overseas operations
   b) Child labor is a major & pervasive problem in the U.S. today
   c) Agriculture is an industry in which child labor is often exploited in other countries
   d) Child labor has very little instrumental value in most developing countries

Sample true-false items:

1) The book, "Mental health of the industrial worker" was credited with making occupational health a legitimate area of study for I/O psychology. T-or-F

2) The positive form of stress is referred to as eustress. T-or-F

3) An important property of the person as a stress mediator is social support. T-or-F

4) In terms of rotating shift work, forward rotation is generally harder for workers to adjust to than backward rotation. T-or-F

5) The FLSA provides legal protection for children in the U.S. in regards to employment. T-or-F

Sample short-answer questions:

1) Describe five of the nine environmental influences on mental health.

2) Contrast the three conceptual models on the relationship between work and family.

3) What are the intended and unintended consequences of employment?

<u>Answer key to the multiple-choice items</u>	<u>Answer key to true-false items</u>
1) c	1) T
2) a	2) T
3) b	3) F
4) c	4) F
5) b	5) T

6) c
7) b
8) d
9) c
10) c

Chapter 12: Study Guide

WORK MOTIVATION

Chapter 12: Outline

Work motivation

    Direction

    Intensity

    Persistence / Duration

Five critical concepts

    Behavior

    Performance

    Ability

    Situational constraints

    Motivation

Work motivation theories

Need hierarchy theory (Maslow)

    Five needs

        Physiological

        Safety

        Social

        Self-esteem

Self-actualization

Three implications of the need hierarchy

Implications for work behavior

Empirical tests of the theory

Evaluation of the theory

Equity theory (Adams)

Social comparison theory

Four parts

Person

Other

Inputs

Outputs

Equity v. inequity

Underpayment

Overpayment

Empirical tests of the theory

Evaluation of the theory

Expectancy theory (Vroom)

    Cognitive theory

    Five parts

        Job outcomes

        Valence

        Instrumentality

        Expectancy

        Force

    Empirical tests of the theory

        Across-subjects design

        Within-subjects design

    Evaluation of the theory

Reinforcement theory (Skinner)

    Operant conditioning / behaviorism

    Three key variables

        Stimulus

        Response

        Reward

    Four types of response-reward contingencies

        Fixed interval

        Fixed ratio

Variable interval

Variable ratio

Empirical tests of the theory

Evaluation of the theory

Goal-setting theory (Locke & Latham)

Two major functions of goals

Basis for motivation

Direct behavior

Two conditions for goal-setting to be effective

Awareness

Acceptance

Factors that influence goal-setting effectiveness

Goal difficulty

Goal specificity

Feedback

Empirical tests of the theory

Evaluation of the theory

Self-regulation theory

    Family of theories

    Major components

        Goals

        Self-monitoring or self-evaluation

        Role of feedback

        Self-efficacy

        Goal revision

    Empirical tests of the theory

        Learning goal orientation v. performance goal orientation

    Evaluation of the theory

Work design theory

    Job design

    Job enrichment

    Job Characteristics Model

        Skill variety

        Task identity

        Task significance

        Autonomy

        Task feedback

Three critical psychological states

    Experienced meaningfulness

    Experienced responsibility

    Knowledge of results of work activities

Personal and work outcomes

Growth-need strength

Motivating potential score

Empirical tests of the theory

Evaluation of the theory

Overview and synthesis of work motivation theories

Distal construct theories

Proximal construct theories

Genetic bases of motivation

    Conscientiousness

"Saving face"

Karoshi

D4DR

Application of motivational strategies

Three determinants of human behavior

Four strategies to motivation

186

Five Critical Concepts of Work Motivation

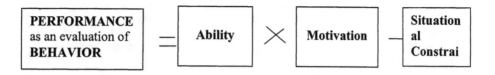

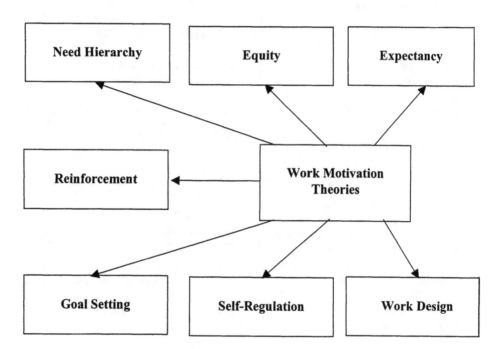

Key Concepts in the Work Motivation Theories

Need Hierarchy Theory

5 needs: physiological, safety, social, self-esteem, & self-actualization

Importance of the hierarchy

Equity Theory

Social comparison

Person: Other - Inputs: Outputs

Equity & Inequity

Expectancy Theory

Outcomes
Valence
Instrumentality
Expectancy
Force

Reinforcement Theory

Stimulus-response-reward

4 contingencies: fixed interval, fixed ratio, variable interval, variable ratio

Goal-setting Theory

Basis & direction of motivation

Awareness & acceptance

Difficulty, specificity & feedback

Self-Regulation Theory

Goals
Self-monitoring or self-evaluation
Role of feedback
Self-efficacy
Goal revision

Word Design Theory

Job enrichment
Job Characteristics Model
    5 characteristics
    3 psychological states
    Personal & work outcomes

Other motivational concepts

Distal v. proximal theories
Genetic basis for motivation
Saving face
Karoshi
D4DR

Web Sites for Chapter 12

1) http://www.ship.edu/~cgboeree/maslow.html

   This web site provides detailed information on Maslow's Need Hierarchy Theory as well as background information on Abraham Maslow and other aspects of his writings.

2) http://www.dushkin.com/connectext/psy/ch09/workmot.mhtml

   This web site is an article on work motivation. It presents a well-known theory on work motivation that is not discussed in the chapter.

3) http://www.japan-101.com/culture/karoshi.htm

   This web site provides information of karoshi.

4) http://quotations.about.com/cs/inspirationquotes/a/Work11.htm

   This web site provides inspirational quotes on the topic of work motivation.

5) http://www.ornl.gov/sci/techresources/Human_Genome/home.shtml

   At the end of this chapter the genetic basis of motivation are discussed in the context of the mapping of the human genome (D4DR). This web site provides information on the human genome project.

This chapter addresses the various perspectives and complexities of work motivation. One of the most important points of this chapter is the relationship between performance and motivation. Too often people assume that your performance on a given task is the sole result of your motivation (you did well because you're a "hard worker" or you did poorly because you're "lazy"). As the text points out, there are other factors that influence your performance. Your ability to perform a task has a substantial impact on your performance. Situational factors (e.g., time limitations, poor equipment, reward system, leadership effectiveness, coworkers/peers) also influence your performance. Thus, performance is a result of your ability and your motivation, hindered by situational constraints. A mathematical representation of this relationship could be:

Performance = (Ability x Motivation) - Situational constraints

It's a multiplicative relationship because if one has limited ability (near "0") or almost no motivation (near "0"), performance will be almost nonexistent (near "0"). The highest performance will occur by an individual with high ability and high motivation and a supportive task environment (no situational constraints).

This exercise requires you to apply this formula to two situations. After completing the exercise, you should have a better grasp of the complexities in the relationship between performance and motivation.

Situation #1: This Course

At the end of this semester you will receive some grade in this course. The grade you receive represents your performance. Answer the questions below.

Performance in this course will be affected by:

a) Which **abilities** are needed to do well in this course?

b) **Motivation:** Why do you want to do well in this course?

c) What **situational constraints** might affect your grade?

d) Based upon your responses, what grade do you expect to receive in this course? Why?

Situation #2: Your job performance

Think about your current job or a job you have recently been employed in. Your performance on that job was/will be appraised in some manner (either formally or informally). Answer the questions below.

Job Performance (measured by):

a) Which **abilities** are needed to do well on this job?

b) **Motivation**: Why do you want do well in this job?

c) What **situational constraints** might affect your job performance?

d) Taking into account the above information, the performance evaluation you expect to receive in this job is (explain):

The majority of this chapter is devoted to the 7 main theories of work motivation: Need Hierarchy, Equity, Expectancy, Reinforcement, Goal-Setting Theory, Self-Regulation Theory and Job Characteristics Theory. The following case study requires you to apply your knowledge of these theories. The goal of this exercise is to enhance your understanding of the major theoretical perspectives on work motivation.

What About Bob?

Bob Blakeslee is an attorney for the law firm of Lye, Cheet, and Steel. He's been employed with the firm for the past 10 years. When he started working there, he set a goal to become a senior partner before his 40th birthday. Last month he found out he's not going to accomplish his goal. The firm decided to promote Roberta James instead. The chances of another senior partner position opening up within the next 5 years is very slim.

Bob and Roberta starting working at Lye, Cheet, and Steel at about the same time. Both Bob and Roberta graduated from the same law school, and had comparable academic accomplishments. Bob was told in his interview that promotion to senior partner would be based strictly upon how much revenue he could generate. Bob worked extremely hard to maintain a high number of "billable hours" per week. Bob would work 70 to 75 hours per week to maintain 50 to 55 billable hours per week (note: billable hours refer to time which a law firm can charge their clients). The firm charges clients $200 per hour for Bob's time. Roberta also desired senior partnership. She also put in comparable hours per week.

Bob took the news of Roberta's promotion pretty hard. Since the announcement of Roberta's promotion, Bob has been late to work 3 times. He's left work early on numerous occasions. His billable hours have averaged only 31 per week over the last month. To top it all off, one of Bob's new clients took his business elsewhere because he did not appreciate Bob's poor attitude. The loss of this client was estimated to cost the company $100,000 per year.

These recent developments in Bob's performance have not gone unnoticed. Brandon Cheet, one of the firm's senior partners, called Bob into his office to discuss these undesirable trends.

Brandon: "Bob, we noticed your performance has slipped quite a bit over the last few weeks. Is anything wrong?"

Bob: "I'm disgusted with my job. I can't believe I didn't get promoted."

Brandon: "Bob, the firm has always been very impressed with you. We think of you as a valuable asset to our company. The choice between you and Roberta was very difficult. It was virtually a tie."

Bob: "I have nothing against Roberta. She's a great lawyer. But I figure what's the point of killing myself. I work as hard as Roberta, but now she has the corner office, the company car, her name on the door, and the title. Why should I care anymore? It's probably going to be 10 more years before anyone else gets promoted."

Brandon: "I'm sorry to hear you feel this way. The people here like you quite a
bit."

Bob: "I know they do. I have a lot of friends here. I really feel like I belong here, but I need more than that. The promotion would have meant respect. Plus it would have given me the opportunity for more challenging cases. I felt like the promotion was the ticket I needed to really become one of the best lawyers around."

Brandon: "I'm sorry you didn't get the promotion, but I believe we made the right decision. The partners still value you very much, but if you don't get out of this funk you're in, you are going to force us to make another decision. So, please snap out of it before something drastic has to happen."

Bob: "Sure."

Bob left Brandon's office. On his way back to his office, a co-worker stopped him and asked how the meeting went with Brandon. Bob replied "It was a complete waste." Bob went home early that day.

Questions:

1) Which motivation theories are applicable to this case? Explain your answer.

2) If you were a senior partner in this firm, what would you do to increase Bob's motivation? Explain your response in the context of a theory (or theories).

3) If you were Bob, what could you do to increase your motivation? Explain.

Exercise 12-3: College Life

As you know this chapter focuses on motivation. Motivation directs our behavior. In the numerous motivation theories presented in this chapter on motivation, the importance of the product of our motivation was critical in many of these theories. For example, for need hierarchy theory the **direction** of behavior is to satisfy needs. For equity theory, motivation is affected by "outcomes" received by the employee (equitable?). Expectancy theory states that outcomes have valences for employees. In goal-setting theory the objective of motivation is to accomplish one's goal. A similar objective is present in self-regulation theory. In this exercise you will first rank order various outcomes associated with college. Using the scale below rank order the following outcomes.

1 = most important, 2 = 2nd most important , …. 7 = least important

When I leave this college/university the outcome that matters most to me is…

_____ I have a high g.p.a. and/or class rank

_____ I have a good job to go to after graduation

_____ I have developed the necessary skills to be successful in my career

_____ I have made some quality friendships that I hope will last a long time

_____ I have found someone to share the rest of my life with intimately

_____ I really enjoyed this part of my life

_____ I know a lot more now than I thought I would

When examining your rankings above you should have a good idea how motivation provides **direction** to your behavior as a college student. The next component of motivation is "intensity." Using the scale below rate your **intensity** for each <u>outcome over the past week.</u>

When I reflect back on the past week I have spent:

1= virtually no time on meeting this objective
2 = a little time on meeting this objective
3 = some time on meeting this objective
4 = a considerable amount of time meeting this objective
5 = virtually all my time meeting this objective

_____ I have a high g.p.a. and/or class rank

_____ I have a good job to go to after graduation

_____ I have developed the necessary skills to be successful in my career

_____ I have made some quality friendships that I hope will last a long time

_____ I have found someone to share the rest of my life with intimately

_____ I really enjoyed this part of my life

_____ I know a lot more know than I thought I would

1) When you compare your ranking to these ratings are there any surprises? In other words are there outcomes that you ranked high that received a low rating or vice versa?

2) Why do you think there are some discrepancies between the rankings and the ratings?

The last major component of motivation is **persistence**. The following questions target this aspect of motivation.

1) When you think back to when you graduated from high school, which of the above mentioned outcomes would have been ranked higher? Why the change?

2) Which would have been ranked lower? Why?

3) Over your college career which of the following outcomes do you think you have been most consistently pursuing? In other words which outcomes have you been the most persistence about?

4) Overall when you think about your responses through this exercise what does it tell you about motivation?

5) Similarly, it is likely that if you shared your responses with other members of the class you will find large differences across the group. What implication does this have for organizations that want to maximize employee motivation?

Sample multiple-choice items:

1) Which component of motivation relates to the potential to exert various levels of effort?

   a) duration
   c) endurance

   b) intensity
   d) direction

2) Research on Expectancy Theory has shown all of the following EXCEPT:

   a) the theory is more predictive of individual preferences rather than identifying one's level of motivation
   b) the theory applies best to people who perceive the ability to control their levels of job performance
   c) people vary significantly in the extent to which their behavior is motivated by rational processes
   d) the theory is more applicable to people that are highly emotional than highly rational

3) If a student sets a goal for this semester "to do his/her best," Goal-Setting Theory would criticize this goal because:

   a) it lacks specificity
   c) it's too difficult

   b) it's not challenging
   d) it's too brief

4) Research on Equity Theory has shown:

   a) that employees are very sensitive to feeling overpaid
   b) that equity principles do not apply to non-monetary outcomes
   c) employees differ in their sensitivity to inequity
   d) social comparisons have limited relevance to motivation

5) According to Need Hierarchy Theory, employees:

   a) focus on relationships with coworkers before concerns with pay and benefits
   b) want opportunities for advancement/growth once their social needs are met
   c) are really only concerned about pay and benefits, everything else is unimportant
   d) can be completely satisfied once they feel that they fit into the organization

6) Paying employees an hourly wage would be an example of a _____ schedule, whereas paying employees for each unit produced would be an example of a _____ schedule.

a) variable interval; variable ratio
b) fixed ratio; variable ratio
c) fixed interval; variable interval
d) fixed interval; fixed ratio

7) All of the following are components of Self-Regulation theory EXCEPT:

a) people consciously set goals
b) feedback is critical
c) task significance improves employee motivation
d) self-efficacy affects one's self-confidence

8) According to the Job Characteristics Theory, which job characteristic refers to the degree to which a job requires a completion of a whole (from beginning to end) piece of work?

a) task identity
b) task significance
c) autonomy
d) task variety

9) All of the following theories are proximal theories EXCEPT:

a) goal-setting theory
b) need hierarchy theory
c) expectancy theory
d) self-regulation theory

10) Based upon research on work motivation, all of the following are true EXCEPT:

a) there is no one "best" motivational theory
b) there are individual differences in motivation
c) work motivation is comparable across cultures
d) external factors (e.g., job, company) can critically affect work motivation

Sample true-false items:

1) Work motivation can be directly observed. T-or-F

2) Equity theory is based upon social comparisons. T-or-F

3) Operant conditioning is another term for self-regulation. T-or-F

4) In the Job Characteristics Model a motivating potential score refers to the motivating properties of a job. T-or-F

5) Karoshi is a Japanese term for "saving face." T-or-F

Sample short-answer questions:

1) Discuss the interplay among motivation, situational constraints and ability in relation to employee performance.

2) In what way are Need Hierarchy Theory and Reinforcement Theory alike and in what way are they are different?

3) Compare and contrast Goal-Setting Theory and Self-Regulation Theory.

Answer key to the multiple-choice items	Answer key to true-false items
1) b	1) F
2) d	2) T
3) a	3) F
4) c	4) T
5) b	5) F
6) d	
7) c	
8) a	
9) b	
10) c	

Chapter 13: Outline

Leadership v. management / administration

Major topics in leadership research

    Positional power

    The leader

    The led

    The influence process

        Coercion

        Manipulation

        Authority

        Persuasion

        Instrumental leadership

        Supportive leadership

    The situation

    Leader emergence v. leader effectiveness

Theoretical approaches to leadership

The trait approach

Individual traits

　　Examples of key traits

　　Personality variables

　　Physical characteristics

　　Role of the situation and individual traits

Motivation (McClelland)

　　Need for power

　　Need for achievement

　　Need for affiliation

The behavioral approach

Two basic behavioral dimensions (Ohio State University research)

　　Initiating structure

　　Consideration

　　Leader Behavior Description Questionnaire

　　Leader Practices Inventory

Specific leader behaviors

　　Monitoring

　　Clarifying

The power and influence approach

Power and leader effectiveness

Power bases (French & Raven)

Reward

Coercive

Legitimate

Expert

Referent

Influence outcomes

Commitment

Compliance

Resistance

Leader-Member Exchange Theory (LMX)

Classifying subordinates based on:

Perceived competence

Trust

Motivation for greater responsibility

In-group v. out-group

Differences in treatment

Psychological bases for the exchange

Personal contribution

Idolized by followers

Blind loyalty and obedience

Appealing vision

"Staging"

Negative charismatics

Implicit leadership theory

Attribution theory of leadership / Social Information Processing Theory

"The romance of leadership"

Substitutes for leadership

Environmental sources that provide direction and structure to employees

Job itself

Technology

Work unit

Leader

Self-leadership

Points of convergence among approaches

Importance of influencing and motivating

Importance of maintaining effective relations

Importance of making decisions

E-leadership

Supply chain management

Cross-cultural leadership issues

GLOBE

Five major findings of GLOBE

In some cultures the concept of leadership is denigrated

Twenty-two universally desirable leadership traits

Eight universally undesirable leadership traits

Many leadership traits were culturally contingent

Members of different culture have similar views on leadership

Self-protective leadership style

Diversity issues in leadership

Gender differences in leadership

Concluding comments - Motivation to lead

Perceived leadership skills or qualities

Agreeable disposition

Sense of social duty and obligation

Concept Charts for Chapter 13

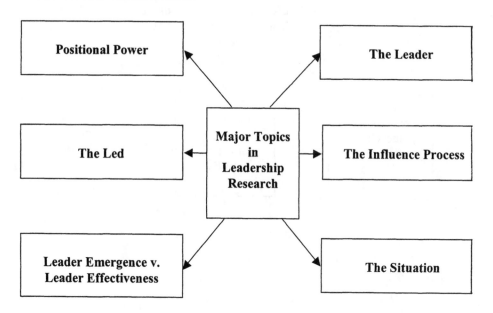

Positional Power

The Leader

The Led

Major Topics in Leadership Research

The Influence Process

Leader Emergence v. Leader Effectiveness

The Situation

Theoretical Approaches to Leadership

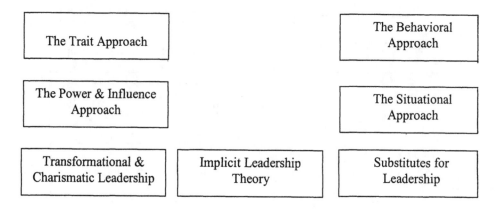

The Trait Approach

The Behavioral Approach

The Power & Influence Approach

The Situational Approach

Transformational & Charismatic Leadership

Implicit Leadership Theory

Substitutes for Leadership

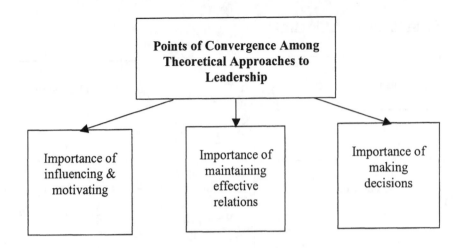

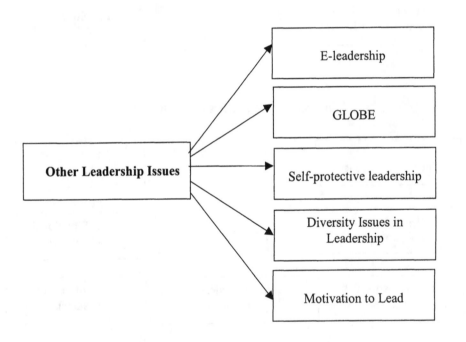

Web Sites for Chapter 13

1) http://www.ccl.org/

This is the web site for the Center for Creative Leadership.

2) http://www.emergingleadership.com/

This is the web site of the Center for Emerging Leadership.

3) http://www.ucalgary.ca/mg/GLOBE/Public/index.htm

This is the home page for the GLOBE project discussed in the chapter.

4) http://www.mindgarden.com/products/mlq.htm

This is the home page for the Multifactor Leadership Questionnaire that was discussed in this chapter.

5) http://www.whitehouse.gov/history/presidents/

A person that often comes to mind when we hear the word "leadership" is a president of the United States. This web site provides information on all U.S. presidents.

Prior to this year, the company you work for distributed a share of their profits with all of the employees equally. This practice, however, has consistently received numerous complaints from employees. A sample of these complaints are: "I've been here 30 years, I should get a bigger bonus than a new guy," "I'm a hell of a worker, why should a marginal performer get as much as me," "I have three kids and two ex-wives to support, that should count for something," and "My job is very important to the success of this firm, why should I get the same bonus as every peon we employ in this place." The company is getting fed up with these complaints. It has decided to create employee problem-solving groups to handle this situation.

You are part of one of these employee problem-solving groups. Most of the other groups have differentially weighted certain factors in their final awards, whereas a few groups have maintained the equal split. Your group has $10,000 to distribute among 6 employees. Your group decision will be binding for this year. The six employees are:

Billy Ray Roberts: 46 years old, salary = $18,000/year, 9 years with the firm, Custodian, married with 5 kids, satisfactory performer. He has grumbled numerous times about needing more money to support his family (good chance he would quit if he could find something better paying, which is possible).

Hilda Frummple: 63 years old, salary = $31,000/year, 38 years with the firm, Secretary, widow, marginal performer. She will be retiring soon. She loves the company, and employees adore her in spite of the fact she has not done a great job of keeping up with technological advances pertinent to her position.

Sherry Cordova: 27 years old, salary = $28,000/year, 2 years with the firm, Assistant Manager, single, excellent performer. She has been very impressive in her brief time in the company. She has the potential to move up quite rapidly in the company if she decides to stay (the job market, however, is quite good for her if she decides to look for employment elsewhere).

Simon Schuster: 54 years old, salary = $63,000/year, 27 years with the firm, Department Head, married with two kids in college, performance is debatable. The employees that work for him can't stand him. He is autocratic and verbally abusive at times. Turnover in his department is the highest in the firm, however departmental productivity is acceptable. He is a powerful individual within the firm; he is not the kind of person you want against you.

Carlos Menendez: 39 years old, salary = $35,000/year, 6 years with the firm, Computer Programmer, married, marginal performer, He is not well liked among his coworkers. Carlos believes this is because he is Hispanic. His wife is an attorney specializing in employment law. Carlos has a strong feeling that he is going to be discriminated against.

Lisa Cortland: 45 years old, salary = $40,000/year, 18 years with the firm, Manager, divorced, excellent performer. She has been consistently impressive. Her co-workers and subordinates think she is one of the best employees at the company.

Results:

What did your group decide? Be prepared to defend your answers.

Billy Ray Roberts	_____
Hilda Frummple	_____
Sherry Cordova	_____
Simon Schuster	_____
Carlos Menendez	_____
Lisa Cortland	_____
TOTAL	**$10,000**

Questions:

1. One of the key issues in this chapter is leader emergence. Did a leader(s) emerge in your group?

2. What traits do you think this person(s) possesses that enabled him/her to emerge as a leader?

3. In this situation, what traits and/or behaviors do you think are necessary for effective leadership?

4. Lastly, the chapter discusses that in some situations appointed leaders are not needed. Do you think this class exercise needed an appointed leader? Explain.

Exercise 13-2: The Big Cheese

As you know this chapter discusses numerous important issues and concepts related to leadership. One of the best ways to learn about leadership, as well most others areas, is through practical experience. This exercise requires you to reflect back upon your own experiences with a leader. By applying your experiences to the following questions you will gain a more thorough command of the issues pertinent to leadership.

Part 1: Your Experiences: Think of a job you have had or a group that you belonged to that had a leader you respected. Keep in mind a leader could be anyone from the CEO of the organization, to your immediate supervisor, to a coworker, to a club president. Keep this person and this situation in mind as you answer the following questions.

Leader's job title?

_____

Part 2: Chapter Material

a) What **traits** did this person demonstrate that made him/her an effective leader?

b) What **behaviors** did this person exhibit as an effective leader?

c) Using French & Raven's 5 **bases of power**, which base(s) of power did this person rely on the most to influence others?

d) Which **influence tactics** did this person rely on as well?

e) Which **situational factors** affected this person's leadership style?

Part 3: Application of Chapter Concepts

a) Why do you think he/she was an effective leader?

b) Do you think this person would be an effective leader in most situations? Explain.

210

c) How important do you think leadership is to the success of an organization?

Exercise 13-3: Leadership & Learning

Chapter 13 presents numerous theories on leadership. This exercise is designed to help you further understand the similarities and differences among these theories by applying your knowledge of these theories to a situation common to the entire class. The common situation which this exercise refers to is the relationship between a teacher and his/her students, which does have commonalties to the relationship between a leader and his/her followers.

1) In what way(s) can a teacher be considered a leader?

2) A teacher could have at his/her disposal all 5 **bases of power** identified by French and Raven. Which bases of power do you think are most effective for a teacher to achieve desired outcomes (e.g., students learn, they are interested in course material, they perform well on tests)?

3) Apply the **Path-Goal** theory to the relationship between a teacher and his/her students.

4) When you think of your favorite teacher, would you consider this person a **transformational** leader or a **charismatic** leader? Explain.

5) Apply **Leader-Member Exchange** theory to the relationship between a teacher and his/her students.

6) Do you think a teacher's leadership style should vary based upon: (explain)

   a) size of the class (20 v. 200)?

   b) level of the course (freshman-level v. senior-level)?

   c) course content (organic chemistry v. intro. to psychology v. poetry)?

   d) student ability (remedial section v. honors section)?

7) If yes, to any or all of the above, what does this tell you about effective leadership?

Sample multiple-choice items:

1) The difference in power between a superior and a subordinate is referred to as:

   a) referent power   b) personal power
   c) positional power   d) implied power

2) As a supervisor Jack is very good at acknowledging his subordinates' needs and concerns, whereas Jill as a supervisor is very good at articulating the group's direction and goals. In sum Jack illustrates ___ leadership and Jill illustrates ___ leadership.

   a) democratic; directive
   b) instrumental; directive
   c) supportive; instrumental
   d) supportive; directive

3) If you examine leadership based upon the leader's personality and integrity, then you are taking a(n) ___ approach to studying leadership.

   a) behavioral
   b) transformational
   c) implicit
   d) trait

4) As managers Michael and Rachel are quite different. Michael emphasizes "getting the job done on time" whereas Rachel believes in employee commitment. According to the behavioral approach to leadership Michael would score high in __ and Rachel would score high in ___.

   a) task dominance; agreeableness
   b) initiating structure; consideration
   c) need for achievement; need for affiliation
   d) time orientation; satisfaction orientation

5) Which power base refers specifically to the authority in one's job title?

   a) reward   b) legitimate
   c) coercive   d) referent

6) Which statement best describes LMX theory?

   a) leaders classify subordinates into two groups: the in-group and the out-group
   b) leaders provide direction and support to help subordinates reach a goal
   c) effective leaders are motivated, expressive and loyal to their subordinates
   d) all of the above are characteristics of LMX theory

7) If you believe that good leaders are those that motivate their employees to accomplish valued objectives, then you most likely believe in the ___ theory of leadership.

   a) Transformational
   b) Path-goal
   c) LMX
   d) Implicit

8) As the company's president Laurie Reynolds does a great job providing support and encouragement to others. Basically she empowers others in the organization to reach their potential. Laurie can be classified as a(n) ___ leader.

   a) implicit
   b) LMX type
   c) transformational
   d) charismatic

9) Besides the leader, there are three other environmental sources that provide direction and structure to employees. Which of the following is NOT one of these sources?

   a) job itself
   b) technology
   c) work unit
   d) competitors

10) All of the following are major findings from the GLOBE project EXCEPT:

   a) Leadership as a concept is universally appreciated across cultures
   b) There are numerous desirable leadership traits across cultures
   c) There are numerous undesirable leadership traits across cultures
   d) People from the same culture often have similar views on leadership

Sample true-false items:

1) McClelland's theory on leader motivation falls under the trait approach to leadership. T-or-F

2) The most positive influence outcome is compliance. T-or-F

3) Path-Goal theory is an example of the behavioral approach to studying leadership.
   T-or-F

4) Implicit leadership theory states that leadership really does not really exist but rather it is a concept we use to attach to certain outcomes. T-or-F

5) In terms of e-leadership it is critical to strengthen your organization's position in the supply-chain of commerce. T-or-F

Sample short-answer questions:

1) What is the difference between leadership and management?

2) Differentiate among LMX theory, path-goal theory, and transformational leadership theory.

3) What is self-protective leadership?

Answer key to the multiple-choice items   **Answer key to true-false items**

1) c   1) T
2) c   2) F
3) d   3) F
4) b   4) T
5) b   5) T
6) a
7) b
8) c
9) d
10) a

Chapter 14: Outline

I/O psychology and union/management relations

Mutual indifference

Taylorism

We/they perspective

Union

Advantages of unionization to employees

Unions as organizations

Large unions in the U.S.

Local union v. national union

Shop (or Union) steward

Union dues

Formation of a union

Union solicitation

Union campaigning

Authorization cards

National Labor Relations Board (NLRB)

Union election

Employee's decision to accept/reject the union

Union instrumentality

The labor contract

Bombast

Negotiating teams

Five key issues

Compensation and working conditions

Employee security

Union security

Management rights

Contract duration

Contract ratification

Bargaining zone

Collective bargaining and impasse resolution

Distributive bargaining

Integrative bargaining

Impasse

Mediation

Federal Mediation and Conciliation Service (FMCS)

Mediator

Fact-finding

    Public sector v. private sector

Arbitration

    Interest arbitration

    American Arbitration Association (AAA)

    Voluntary arbitration

    Compulsory arbitration

    Conventional arbitration

    Final-offer arbitration

    Narcotic effect of arbitration

Responses to impasse

Strikes

    Scheduling of strikes

    "Scabs"

    Strike fund

    Stockpiling goods

Work slowdowns

    "Blue flu"

Sabotage

Lockout

Grievances

Grievance procedure

Grievance arbitration

Grievances as an index of the quality of union/management relations

Factors affecting filing of grievances

Alternative dispute resolution

Influence of unions on nonunionized companies

Union/nonunion wage differential

National Labor Relations Act

Employee support for unions

Dissatisfaction with employment conditions

Union influence

Institutional socialization

Individual socialization

Dispute settlement

Hybrid method

Commitment to the union (union loyalty)

Dual allegiance

Union density

Union instrumentality

Union ideology

Typology of union member's commitment to the union

    Alienated member

    Instrumental member

    Ideological member

    Devoted member

I/O psychology and industrial relations

Personnel selection

    Union shops

        Right-to-work laws

    Open and agency shops

    Union influence

    Qualified seniority in promotions

Personnel training

    Apprenticeship

    Bureau of Apprenticeship and Training

Leadership development

    Procedural justice and OCB

Employee involvement

    Impact on we/they attitudes

Organizational change

    Role of the labor contract

Concluding comments

Traditional objectives of unions

Bargain collectively with employers

Political activity

Generate new members and increase revenue from dues

Concept Charts for Chapter 14

The Formation of a Union

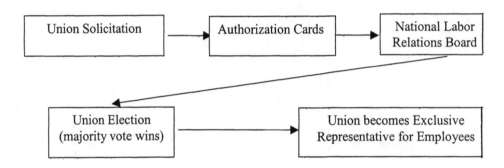

Compensation & Working Conditions	**Five Key Issues of a Labor Contract**	Employee Security
Union Security	Management Rights	Contract Duration

Responses to an Impasse in Collective Bargaining

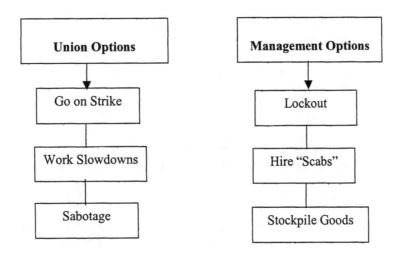

I/O Psychology and Industrial Relations

Personnel Selection	Personnel Training	Leadership Development	Employee Involvement	Organizational Change
Union shops	Apprentice-ship	Procedural justice & OCB	Impact on we/they attitudes	Role of the labor contract
Open & agency shops				
Union influence				
Qualified seniority				

Web Sites for Chapter 14

1) http://www.aflcio.org/

The text mentions some of the largest unions in the U.S. This is the web site for the AFL-CIO, which is one of these unions.

2) http://www.nlrb.gov/

This is the web site for the National Labor Relations Board, which is the primary federal agency that addresses union issues in business.

3) http://www.ilr.cornell.edu/

If you are interested in pursuing a career in union/management relations, this web site describes one of our nation's top programs for this area of study.

4) http://www.teamster.org/

This is the Teamster's web site.

5) http://www.uaw.org/

This is the web site for the United Auto Workers.

Exercise 14-1: Wheelin' & Dealin'

This exercise will give you a small taste of union/management negotiations. Your instructor will assign you to either role play a union negotiator or a management negotiator. You will bargain over 4 issues that are typically discussed in collective bargaining. There are two conditions that you need to be aware of:

1. You have a duty of "good faith bargaining" (as required by law). Thus, you can't lie, cheat, or refuse to negotiate with the other party.

2. The company has been and most likely will remain unionized for quite some time. Therefore, it is important for both parties, not only to reach an agreement that will satisfy their constituents, but also to maintain some type of relationship with the other party.

Background information: The company, the Marion Monitor Manufacturing Company (MMM), produces monitors for computers of all sizes, shapes, and models. The company was highly profitable in the 1980s, however due to increased competition, both foreign and domestic, the company's profits have steadily decreased. Nonetheless, the company is still making a rather hefty profit each year. The company fears that if it doesn't "tighten its belt," the company could be in serious financial trouble in a few years. The company would like to regain its status as the leader in monitor manufacturing. The union, the United Monitor Workers (UMW), would like very much to see the workers at MMM be compensated comparably to other members of UMW. The union feels that MMM does not share the profits adequately with their employees and thus MMM employees are paid well below other unionized monitor manufacturing employees. Below are the revenues and expenses for the company for the last five years:

YEAR	Revenues	Expenses
2000	$29.7 million	$21.1 million
2001	$33.1 million	$25.2 million
2002	$36.6 million	$29.0 million
2003	$37.8 million	$31.6 million
2004	$40.0 million	$34.9 million

Issue #1: **Wages**: *Current average wage at MMM: $10.35/hour*
  Average wage of local nonunionized workers in this industry: $10.25/hour
  Average wage of local unionized workers in this industry: $10.55/hour
  Average wage of unionized workers nationally in this industry: $10.95/hour
  Inflation has increased 5% over the past year.
  Every $.05/hour increase in wages will cost the company $50,000 per year

Issue #2: **Medical benefits**: *Current agreement: employees pay the first $250 of medical expenses per year, after $250 is spent the company pays 80% of the remaining medical bills*
  Typical agreement for nonunionized workers: same
  Typical agreement for local unionized workers: a $150 deductible
  Typical agreement for unionized workers nationally: a $50 deductible
  For every $50 reduction in the deductible will cost the company $20,000 per year

Issue #3: **Holidays & Sick days**: *Current agreement: Employees have 7 paid holidays off and receive 5 sick days per year*
  Typical agreement for nonunionized workers: 5 paid holidays & 5 sick days
  Typical agreement for local unionized workers: 6 paid holidays & 5 sick days
  Typical agreement for unionized workers nationally: 5 paid holidays & 5 sick days
  Every additional day off will cost the company $25,000 per year

Issue #4: **Retirement fund**: *Current agreement: Employer contributes an additional 3% of an employee's income into an investment account (stocks & bonds)*
  Typical agreement for nonunionized workers: 2%
  Typical agreement for local unionized workers: 4%
  Typical agreement for unionized workers nationally: 5%
  Each additional 1% contribution will cost company $75,000 per year

Agreement:
  Issue #1: wages   _____
  Issue #2: medical   _____
  Issue #3: time off   _____
  Issue #4: retirement   _____

TOTAL Cost (or Savings) to employer: _____

Union Side

Issue #1: **Wages**: *Current average wage at MMM: $10.35/hour*
Average wage of local nonunionized workers in this industry: $10.25/hour
Average wage of local unionized workers in this industry: $10.55/hour
Average wage of unionized workers nationally in this industry: $10.95/hour
Inflation has increased 5% over the past year
Every $.05/hour increase in wages will cost the company $50,000 per year

Issue #2: **Medical benefits**: *Current agreement: employees pay the first $250 of medical expenses per year, after $250 is spent the company pays 80% of the remaining medical bills*
Typical agreement for nonunionized workers: same
Typical agreement for local unionized workers: a $150 deductible
Typical agreement for unionized workers nationally: a $50 deductible
For every $50 reduction in the deductible will cost the company $20,000 per year

Issue #3: **Holidays & Sick days**: *Current agreement: Employees have 7 paid holidays off and receive 5 sick days per year*
Typical agreement for nonunionized workers: 5 paid holidays & 5 sick days
Typical agreement for local unionized workers: 6 paid holidays & 5 sick days
Typical agreement for unionized workers nationally: 6 paid holidays & 5 sick days
Every additional day off will cost the company $25,000 per year

Issue #4: **Retirement fund**: *Current agreement: Employer contributes an additional 3% of an employee's income into an investment account (stocks & bonds)*
Typical agreement for nonunionized workers: 2%
Typical agreement for local unionized workers: 4%
Typical agreement for unionized workers nationally: 5%
Each additional 1% contribution will cost company $75,000 per year

Agreement:

Issue #1: wages _____

Issue #2: medical _____

Issue #3: time off _____

Issue #4: retirement _____

TOTAL Cash benefit (or cost) to employees:

_____

Questions: *Please answer the following questions after the negotiations are finished.*

1. What external factors played the biggest role in the negotiations?

2. How would you describe your negotiations? Integrative or distributive?

3. How do you think this style of negotiating will affect future negotiations?

4. How do you think your constituents will react to the agreement you reached?

5. Has your opinion of union/management negotiations changed as a result of this exercise? How?

Exercise 14-2: Clear Contract?

In the previous exercise you negotiated over four issues that often play a key role in collective bargaining. There are other issues that are very important to both union and management that deal with employee discipline. As the chapter points out, in the section entitled "Disputes over Contract Interpretation", grievance arbitration is another critical issue in union/management relations. Listed below are two issues often specified in a union/management contract. A problem occurs in the interpretation of each of them.

Issue #1: Excessive Absenteeism

Policy in the labor contract: *Any employee who is late three times within a three month period will be suspended for one day without pay. The second time this occurs in a three month period the employee is suspended for one week. The third time it occurs, the employee will be terminated.*

Situation: Juanita Romerez has shown up late for work three consecutive days in a row. Her supervisor wants to suspend her for one day as specified in the contract. Juanita has contacted the union steward to represent her to contest this

226

penalty. She knows that she has been late 3 times in a row. However, all three times she has been late by only 5 minutes. Further, Juanita takes the bus to work each day. She takes the first bus the city runs (6:45 a.m.), but the bus doesn't get her to the company until 7:03 a.m. Thus, by the time she punches in she is 5 minutes late. She cannot afford any other way to get to work. Moreover, she feels the policy is unfair because other employees can show up an hour or more late without any penalty unless it happens three times within a three month period. Upon further investigation, the company has found many other employees (predominately minority employees) that start work at 7 a.m. and take the bus to work have also been 5 minutes late consistently. Juanita's supervisor was the first to enforce this policy.

Issue #2: Layoff Policy

Policy in the labor contract: *If a layoff is necessary, management agrees to lay off employees in order of seniority regardless of job performance. Those with the most seniority are the last to be laid off.*

Situation: The company, with union approval, has decided to reduce its labor force across the board by 10% due to reduced consumer demand. The company has gone through its employee roster by job category and has discovered a major problem. There are employees in job categories with less organizational tenure than other employees in that category, but have greater job tenure than other employees. Further, there are employees in different departments with differing levels of tenure.

For example, Larry Logan is a crew chief in the plastics division. He was promoted to crew chief 3 years ago. He has been with the company for 25 years. Jerry Johnson is also a crew chief in the plastics division. However, he was hired in this position 15 years ago. Thus, he has greater job tenure than Larry (15 compared to 3), but less organizational tenure than Larry (15 compared to 25). Who should be let go first in accordance with the policy? Further, Harry Houseman is a crew chief in the rubber division. He has been with the company 7 years, four of which as crew chief. Should Harry be let go before Larry or Jerry even though he is in a different division? There are also plenty of entry-level laborers (positions below crew chief on the organizational chart). Should these employees be factored into to the layoff of crew chiefs? Whoever the company chooses to lay off will most likely contact the union steward to prevent the job loss.

Questions:

1. If you were the arbitrator, how would you resolve each issue? Why?

2. At first glance both policies seem quite clear. From the situations described, however, you can see both issues need to be substantially revised. How would you revise them?

Exercise 14-3: Unionization & I/O Psychology: Stimulus Response

---

You are an I/O psychologist working as an independent consultant. You have been recently contacted by the CEO of a midsize manufacturing firm located in a large metropolitan area. You meet with the CEO later that day to find out he is very concerned about his company becoming unionized. When he pulled into the executive parking lot today, he noticed several employees congregating in the employee lot before work. He sent his assistant out into the employee lot to find out what was going on. The assistant came back with a flyer from a local union that he found on the ground. This union has organized several of the company's competitors in the area and nationwide. The assistant wasn't able to find any employee willing to talk to him to find out what spurred this interest in unionization. All employees denied that they were discussing the formation of a union. The CEO would like your help to prevent the formation of a union in his organization.

1. What information would you want to find out about his company?

2. What information would you want to find out about unionized companies in this industry?

3. What information would you want to find out about this particular union?

4. What are the steps for the formation of a union?

5. What legal activities can management undertake to persuade employees not to unionize?

6. What management activities would be illegal in trying to prevent unionization?

7. What areas of I/O psychology will be affected the most if the company becomes unionized? Explain.

Sample multiple-choice items:

1) The shop steward is:

   a) a management employee that meets regularly with the union representatives
   b) a union member that is responsible for overseeing union growth in a particular industry (e.g., auto manufacturing)
   c) the elected union member that leads the national union
   d) a union employee that is the point person for union activity at the given company

2) To have an union election at least 30% of employee must:

   a) sign authorization cards requesting an election
   b) have prior experience as union members in previous employment
   c) file a grievance of unfair working conditions at the facility
   d) not be classified as management or professional employees

3) If a union is viewed by employees as having great power to improve their working conditions and benefits, then it is said that this union has high:

   a) ratification
   b) authorization
   c) instrumentality
   d) institutional socialization

4) All of the following are key issues in negotiating the labor contract EXCEPT:

   a) contract duration
   b) recruitment practices
   c) management rights
   d) union security

5) Integrative bargaining:

   a) occurs when one side wins and the other side loses
   b) is common in most union negotiations in the U.S.
   c) is characterized by a win-win mentality
   d) occurs when one side has significantly more power than the other side

6) If as an arbitrator you have to pick either the union proposal or the management proposal, then this type of arbitration is called ___ arbitration.

a) compulsory
b) final-offer
c) conventional
d) mandated

7) All of the following are management responses to an impasse EXCEPT:

a) stockpiling of goods
b) lockout
c) hiring of "scabs"
d) sabotage

8) Robert has been a machinist at XYZ company for 30 years. For the last 20 years the company has been unionized. To keep it that way Robert takes new hires out for drinks and tells them of the value of the union to get them to be active in it right away. This scenario is an illustration of ___ socialization.

a) individual
b) institutional
c) organizational
d) informal

9) Open shops, union shops and agency shops are related to which I/O psychology area?

a) training
b) compensation
c) selection
d) development

10) The traditional objectives of unions includes all of the following EXCEPT:

a) increasing revenues from dues
b) political activity promoting worker rights
c) bargain collectively with employers
d) encouraging free trade agreements with foreign countries

Sample true-false items:

1) The government agency most responsible for monitoring union/management relations is the National Federation of Labor Relations. T-or-F

2) A mediator acts as a neutral third party to help unions and management resolve an impasse without the power to enforce the parties to accept an offer. T-or-F

3) The "blue flu" is a negotiating tactic by management that refers to a financial inability to meet union demands (a.k.a. "crying the blues"). T-or-F

4) A common measure of the quality of union/management relations in a company is the number of grievance filed over a given time period. T-or-F

5) Right-to-work laws prohibit union shops in certain states in our country. T-or-F

Sample short-answer questions:

1) Describe the process by which a company typically becomes unionized.

2) Differentiate among mediation, fact-finding and arbitration.

3) Discuss four of the five ways industrial relations can impact I/O psychology.

Answer key to the multiple-choice items	Answer key to true-false items
1) d	1) F
2) a	2) T
3) c	3) F
4) b	4) T
5) c	5) T
6) b	
7) d	
8) a	
9) c	
10) d	